CW00640871

Discover

The Dominican Republic

Cover picture: Palm trees dapple shade on the golden sands, sea and sky are azure-blue — and someone shares it with you. Is this Paradise or just the Caribbean coast of the Dominican Republic?

DOMINICAN ODDITIES

El Malecón. El Malecón is the Dominican-Spanish word for the sea-front boulevard in any coastal town.

Santo Domingo. Dominicans refer to their capital city as *La Capital*, rather than by name. When they say 'Santo Domingo' they are referring to the entire country.

Abbreviations. Towns that are well-known and have long names frequently are referred to on maps and timetables by standard abbreviations, thus:

> Santo Domingo — Sto. Dgo.
> Puerto Plata — Pto. Pta.
> San Pedro de Macoris — S.P.M.

...and San Fco de Macoris is named from Saint Francis — San Fransisco.

Martin Hyde was raised in east Kent within sight of the continent of Europe, a fact that filled him with the desire to travel and understand other cultures. Prepared with a knowledge of Spanish and French as well as English, he has travelled widely in Europe, Africa, Latin America and North America. After graduating in Art and English at Exeter University he worked in Spain, Morocco and the Dominican Republic, spending three years in the latter. Travelling extensively there, he shared his experiences with his Spanish wife Concha and together they pooled their knowledge of the country, its people, and their customs, to produce this book.

Discover
The Dominican
Republic

Martin Hyde

edited by
Terry Palmer

HERITAGE
HOUSE

DISCOVER THE DOMINICAN REPUBLIC
First published March 1990

ISBN 1.85215.019X

Typesetting extrapolated in 8.5 on 9.5 Rockwell on Linotronic 300 by Anglia Photoset, St Botolph St, Colchester, from in-house computer setting.

Printed by Colorcraft Ltd, Whitfield Rd, Causeway Bay, Hong Kong.

Distributed in the UK, Europe, Asia and Australasia by Roger Lascelles, 47 York Rd, Brentford, TW8 0QP.

Distributed in the USA by Boerum Hill Books, Brooklyn, NY 11217-0007.

Published by Heritage House (Publishers) Ltd, Kings Rd, Clacton-on-Sea, CO15 1BG.

© **Martin Hyde, 1990.**

Acknowledgements:

Leoncio Crespo, Director, Dpto Relaciones Internacionales de la Secretaría de Estado de Turismo; Dr José F. López, M.D, Primary Care Medicine — Community Medicine, Sub-director del Centro Médico, Central Romana; James Penn, ornithologist; Rafael Saiz Saviñon, Volare Travels, La Romana; Lic. Grace Guerrero, Técnico Turístico.

CONTENTS

DISCOVER THE DOMINICAN REPUBLIC

KEY TO MAPS

Author Martin Hyde and his Spanish wife Concha.

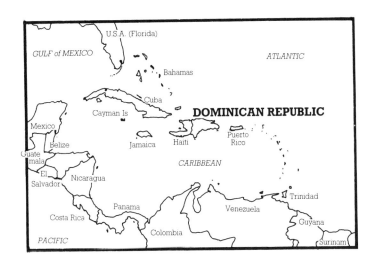

1: WHY THE DOMINICAN REPUBLIC?

Paradise found?

THE DOMINICAN REPUBLIC IS THE CARIBBEAN'S up-and-coming tourist destination. It is the largest country after Cuba in the Caribbean island chain. Its people speak Spanish, and sugar has traditionally been the basis of the economy. Its northern shores are washed by the Atlantic; its southern shores by the Caribbean. It has the highest mountain, the largest lake, the biggest city and arguably the most beautiful beaches in this tropical archipelago. And it has the oldest buildings in the New World, as this was among the islands that Columbus discovered on his maiden voyage of 1492. (See *Discover Florida* in this series for the oldest house in the USA.)

La República Dominicana is formed from two thirds of the island of Hispaniola; the other third is Haiti. Hispaniola lies 50 miles (80km) east of Cuba, and is separated from it by *el Canal del Viento,* the Windward Passage; it is 64 miles (102km) west of Puerto Rico, separated here by *el Canal de la Mona,* the Mona Passage.

The island of Hispaniola thus lies between the two conflicting ideological poles of Communism and Capitalism, yet the Dominican Republic is politically stable compared with the vast majority of Central and South American countries, and for the past 20 years it has achieved stability with free elections and a democratic government.

Where? The Dominican Republic lies between latitudes 17°36′ and 19°59′ N, and between longitudes 68°19′ and 74°38′ W, and has a tropical climate and vegetation. It covers between 18,696 sq miles (48,422 sq km) and 18,816 sq miles (48,734 sq km), including inland waters − opinions differ on the total area − and from east to west stretches to around 240 miles (388km), while in the middle it reaches 170 miles (274km) at its widest point.

The Dominican Republic part of the island of Hispaniola offers a vast range of scenery: in the central highlands it has the Caribbean's highest peak, Pico Duarte, at 10,417ft (3,175m), and the semi-desert south-west has its largest lake, Lago Enriquillo, at 144ft (46m) *below* sea level.

Within 50 miles you can travel from the cactus-infested Enriquillo area to the lush alpine region of the mountains; then there is also the choice of the contrasting coasts, of the Caribbean to the south with its beautiful still waters and palm-fringed beaches, and the rougher, wilder seas and beaches of the Atlantic shores in the north and east. The total length of coastline is 985 miles (1,576km).

Land of contrasts. The contrasts don't stop with the geographical variations this land has to offer; on your holiday you can spend anything from US$2 a night on a room and US$4 a day on food, to US$200, £130, a night and US$100, £65, a day. The Dominican Republic is a country where you can have a really cheap holiday in the sun, or where you can laze in the lap of luxury in one of the top-class resorts such as Casa de Campo in La Romana, or Jack Tar Village in Puerto Plata. The range of choice is vast.

And then there is the fascinating racial mix; there is not a colour or a race that is out of place in the Dominican Republic — and you will see people of every complexion from black to white living in harmony.

The Dominican Republic is easy to reach, having major international airports in the capital, Santo Domingo, and in Puerto Plata; there are smaller international airports serving La Romana and Punta Cana, and one being built at Barahona. Fifteen major airlines serve the country along with the national carrier Dominicana de Aviación, as well as the tour companies' charter flights which operate from countries including Great Britain, Germany and the USA. By air, Santo Domingo is little more than two hours from Miami, five hours from New York, and only 40 minutes from San Juan in Puerto Rico.

What's doing? And when you arrive in the Dominican Republic there is a wealth of things to see and do. You can admire the New World's oldest city, Santo Domingo — its name translates as *Holy Sunday* — and visit Columbus's tomb; or go hiking in one of the national parks and enjoy the natural beauty of the island and its wildlife, which even includes crocodiles. For the outdoor type there are ample opportunities for horse-riding, water sports and scuba diving.

This, then, is the tropical paradise of the Dominican Republic: accessible, relaxing and beautiful, and offering an ideal break from winter's drizzle and snow. On Christmas Day you can be on a sun-soaked beach sipping a piña colada!

You're still not convinced? Here's one overriding reason for choosing this country as opposed to such rivals as Jamaica or Barbados: this is the cheapest isle in the Caribbean and you pay in the local currency, the Dominican peso, not in US dollars as in so many other Carib havens.

2: BEFORE YOU GO

Paperwork and planning

PASSPORTS and VISAS. Every visitor to the Dominican Republic needs a valid pasport, but visas are not required for a stay of up to 90 days by nationals of the UK, Austria, Denmark, Finland, Germany (West), Greece, Italy, Norway, Spain, Switzerland, Sweden, and a number of lesser states.

Tourist card. Visitors from Belgium, Canada, France, Jamaica, Luxemburg, the Netherlands, Portugal, and the USA (including Puerto Rico and the US Virgin Islands) need to buy tourist cards; they are available either in Dominican consulates abroad, through the airline which sells you your ticket, or on arrival. The cost is US$10 for an entitlement of 60 days, and the card can be renewed twice with no extra charge. You must *surrender it when you leave.*

For further information contact La Dirección General de Migración, Departamento de Extranjería, Santo Domingo, The Dominican Republic; ✆685.2505.

Visas for Haiti. Citizens of the USA, Canada, and Western European countries *except* Spain, France and Italy, don't need visas to visit Haiti. Those who do need them must go to the Embajada de Haiti, B. Scout n°11, Santo Domingo, ✆562.3519. The embassy is open from 0900 to 1300 on weekdays; you will need a valid passport, two photographs and US$12.

Climate and weather.

The Dominican Republic has a tropical climate with two **rainy seasons:** the main one is from May to July, but you can also expect rain from November to January when a colder wind blows across the country from the north. The rains are tropical, which means the sun will shine almost every day even at the height of the wet season, and a day of total overcast is rare. Rain usually comes as a short, sharp downpour, forcing people to shelter for a while before they continue with their daily business: if you get caught you can dry out within half an hour.

Rainfall is not evenly spread across the country. The regions of rain shadow are in the south and the north-west, both of which are very dry and look more like southern Morocco than the tropics. On the north-facing slopes of the mountains rain is more frequent and the vegetation here is consequently much greener; near Puerto Plata there are areas that receive more than 94in (2,400mm) of rain a year — but in Montecristi, Azua, Neiba, Jimaní and Pedernales, the annual rainfall is less than 27in (700mm).

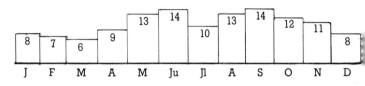

DAYS OF RAIN (per month) in SANTO DOMINGO

Temperatures are fairly constant throughout the year, with a variation of about 5.5°F (3°C), affected only by altitude. For example, Santo Domingo has an average temperature of 75°F (24°C) in January and 80.6°F (27°C) in August, and in high summer Jimaní and Mao can experience 102°F (39°C); heat at this intensity can make sleeping uncomfortable if you're roughing it in cheap hotels without air conditioning or fans, or where · — even with a ceiling fan — the electricity supply may not be maintained throughout the night.

In the mountains in winter you will need a good sweater, as well as a coat and gloves if you're motor-cycling; the temperature won't drop to freezing point but the chill factor may make it feel that cold.

Swimmers will find that the **sea** is warm all the year, the Caribbean being a degree or so warmer than the Atlantic; the average winter sea temperature is 79—81°F (26—27°C) in winter, and 84—88°F (29—31°C) in summer.

When you arrive you may need to adjust, and you might feel slightly more lethargic than usual for a day or so. This is mainly due to the humidity which ranges from 72% to 90%. Although this is high (it shows the percentage of maximum amount of moisture the air can hold at a given temperature), many visitors comment that it is not as oppressive as in other tropical areas.

Hurricanes. Hurricanes are common in the West Indies, and the Dominican Republic has always been a prime target for them. By definition, a hurricane is a wind of greater than 73mph (116.8kph), and it can strike an island with devastating results. People still talk in hushed voices about Hurricane David which hit the country in 1979 killing more than 2,000 people and destroying the homes of 200,000 others, with damage estimated at US$1bn.

Hurricanes have a fascination to anybody who has yet to live through the fury of one, but they are indeed deadly dangerous manifestations of energy. They have their regular season from August through October, and studies have shown that there is a crucial week in which the most dangerous hurricanes have formed: it is from 11 to 18 September, the time when Hurricane Hugo struck Puerto Rico in 1989 but veered to the north of the Dominican Republic. Bear this date in mind when planning your holiday.

A tropical storm has winds less than 30mph (50kph); as its windspeed increases it is upgraded to a cyclone which, by definition, has winds from 30mph to 73mph (50kph to 116.8kph); in excess of this it becomes the dreaded hurricane, and its winds may reach speeds of 200mph (360kph) though the storm as a body moves erratically at relatively low speeds across the Caribbean, often no faster than 6mph (11kph).

Hurricanes are named in alphabetical order each season, beginning with A, the names alternating between male and female, and in meteorological terms each is an enormous mass of air and water vapour that is spiralling around the 'eye' of the storm, an area where pressure is so low that it causes shuttered houses to explode from the greater air pressure inside them; strangely, the air in the eye is usually a dead calm. The lower the pressure, the stronger the winds, and the greater the damage, with the tail winds following the eye being the most treacherous because they strike from the opposite direction and catch many people unaware.

The tropical storm that becomes a hurricane begins life over the Atlantic, often near the bulge of western Africa, and drifts into the Caribbean with the North-East Trades, gaining momentum. The normal hurricane disintegrates when it hits a land mass, but the exception is the one which lives on in memory, such as David, Donna, and in 1989 Hugo.

Hurricanes normally follow a set route which takes them across the Caribbean in a circular sweep, entering from the south-east and leaving to the north-east, with most of those that survive impact with the Lesser Antilles eventually crossing the Greater Antilles − which includes Hispaniola.

Hurricane precautions. The most dangerous place to be in the Dominican Republic during a storm is in the south-west, especially in Barahona. As 90% of deaths are caused by drowning, it's essential to keep well away from the coast and its tidal surge, heading for preference into the mountains. But beware the valleys and gulches, as you could be drowned in the flash-floods brought about by the excessive rain that comes with every hurricane − up to 30 inches

(7,500mm) *a day.*

The US Hurricane Tracking Center in Miami now follows the progress of every tropical storm entering the Caribbean, so there is no possibility of a hurricane striking without warning, but if you are in the country when such a storm is coming, get away from the low-lying coastal areas, stock up with food, drinking water, candles and matches, and stay inside, well away from windows. If you have transport, fill the tank as most gas (petrol) stations are out of action for several days after the impact.

Sunburn. The tropical sunshine will be far more of a threat to you than will any hurricane. As this is indeed the tropics and the sun shines down from a high angle, there is less atmosphere to filter out the more harmful radiation. Sunbathe and tan little by little, and be careful not to overdo it on the first day.

Health care.

No international vaccination certificate is necessary for entering the Dominican Republic. If you come on a package holiday and stay in tourist complexes your chances of catching a serious illness are very rare, and even if you travel independently, staying in local hotels, the chances are still very slim. The World Health Organisation states that the peoples' average health and life expectancy are the same as, if not better than, in the USA. Most of the illness in the Dominican Republic is caused by poverty rather than by a hostile climate.

AIDS. Known in the Spanish-speaking world as SIDA — *síndrome inmunidad deficiencia adquirida* — AIDS has arrived in the republic; according to the Secretary of Public Health there were 821 reported cases by the end of 1988, with 394 of them coming in that year. The government is making an effort to teach the people how to avoid catching the disease, but as we know its cause we should be vigilant.

Dengue. Dengue is a tropical disease transmitted by mosquitos. Its symptoms are headaches, vomiting, coughing, fever, and aching of the bones, but the strain found in the Dominican Republic is not the dangerous type that can lead to haemmorhaging, and need not be feared any more than common 'flu; the treatment is to drink plenty and take Paracetamol or Aspirin.

Diarrhoea. The most common complaint for the visitor is diarrhoea, which may be caused by a variety of factors — change of climate, of food, of water. If you're prone to this debility, take a good stock of anti-diarrhoea medicine, but to avoid contracting it, wash all fruit, avoid eating salads, and drink purified or mineral water. But if you're travelling independently for longish periods in the backwoods, there'll come the occasion when you'll just have to take what's available and suffer a short period of adjustment.

Hepatitis. Hepatitis 'A' and 'B' exist in the republic, although only a

12

few cases of the more dangerous 'B' have been reported. Hepatitis 'A,' the acute infective form, is a virus transmitted by direct contact with the faeces of an infected person through contaminated food or water. Symptoms are a low fever, dark urine, pain in the liver region, and a yellowing of the skin. There is no vaccination, and the cure is a low-fat, high-protein diet, plenty of drink, but no alcohol for three months.

Malaria. There is virtually no malaria in the country, with the possible exception of the southern region by the Haitian frontier. Unless you're visiting this part of the country there is no need to take anti-malarial precautions, but if you plan to go into this area then bring the drugs with you; to be completely effective you must start the course a week before your arrival in the affected region and continue for a month after you leave it.

Schistosomiasis. Schistosomiasis, also known as bilharzia, affects 200,000 people in the tropics. It is caused by schistomes, parasites up to 25mm long which live in semi-stagnant rivers and ponds and whose free-floating eggs enter the body through the skin and infect the blood stream. It's an uncomfortable rather than a potentially fatal disease, and the prevention is simple: don't swim in the rivers of the Eastern Region of the Dominican Republic — and in many other parts of the world.

Typhoid and cholera. There is no risk from typhoid or cholera, and **yellow fever** is not found in the country.

A quiet corner in Altos de Chavón.

Water problems. I recommend you not to drink the tap water, particularly if you're prone to stomach upsets, *unless you know it is purified.* Water is purified in all the tourist hotels and complexes, but outside the tourist circuit caution must prevail. In a local restaurant in Santo Domingo or any other town, it's prudent to opt for a beer or soda water rather than tap water − but if you must have plain water, ask that it be *filtrada* or *purificada.* And don't forget that the ice served in bars is almost certainly not made from *agua purificada.*

The one real problem with drinking water in the Dominican Republic isn't what to do with it when you've got it, but is getting it in the first instance. Most urban Dominicans are without a dependable supply because of the electricity cuts which also stop the pumping stations, and in the villages the children spend all day drawing water from the river as there is no mains supply in any event.

When travelling independently you must expect to turn on taps that remain stubbornly dry, but the rural hotel owner has the answer: he gives you a bucket of water to wash with.

MEDICAL EMERGENCY CENTRES:

24-HOUR SERVICE IN TOURIST AREAS
Barahona:
Hospital Jaime Mota, Ctra. Enriquillo Km2, ✆524.2441.
Hospital Jaime Sánchez, Ctra. Central, ✆524.2505 (Ctra. = Carretera, main road).
La Romana:
Hospital Central Romana, Central Romana, ✆687.7787.
Clínica Canela, Av Libertad 44, ✆556.3135; 556.3874.
Puerto Plata:
Centro Médico Dr Bournigal, Antera Mota, ✆586.2342.
Hospital Ricardo Limardo, J.F.Kunhart, ✆586.2210.
Samaná:
Centro Médico Moratín, ✆583.2233.
Centro Médico San Vicente, ✆538.2535.
Santo Domingo:
Clínica Abreu, Av Independencia, ✆686.8784.
Clínica Chan & Santos, Fantino Falco, 21, ✆567.4421.
Clínica Gómez Patiño, Av Independencia, 701, ✆685.9131.
Santiago:
Hospital José Ma. Cabral y Báez, Central, ✆583.4311.

Anybody going on holiday to the Dominican Republic should carry full medical insurance. It's worth knowing that many doctors in the country speak English, as they have studied in the USA.

Indian ghosts reappear in solid form at a stall selling soapstone carvings.

Dangerous creatures and pests.

On land. The *araña* or *cacata*, is a beautiful spider as big as an outstretched hand, which appears mostly from September to December. The English-speaking world calls it the tarantula, but this name strictly applies to the much smaller and more venomous spider found in the Taranto region of Italy. The *araña* — it just means 'spider' — is a peaceful creature that will jump at you only if provoked, but its bite causes high fever and can be fatal for babies.

Another dangerous creature is the **centipede**, *ciempies*, (not a misprint), which in the Dominican Republic is orange and around eight inches (20cm) long. Its bite has been known to kill adults but as it's a rare creature don't expect to see one.The **scorpion**, *alacrán*, is also very rare, and there are no dangerous snakes at all on Hispaniola.

In the sea. The most dangerous creatures of the sea aren't the big ones. **Sharks**, *tiburones*, will attack man but they are not a problem for bathers as they prefer to be in the Mona Passage where there are big fish for them to feed on. The more realistic dangers come from less spectacular creatures such as the **stone fish** which has in its dorsal fin a poisonous spine that can inflict intense pain and cause a severe fever if stepped on; some relief comes from washing the wound in water.

The **jellyfish**, *medusa* or *agua viva,* can be a problem, particularly the Portuguese man-o'-war and the sea wasp; the latter is difficult to see in water and has long and highly-venomous tentacles; the sting itself isn't the killer, but it can induce shock and consequent death by drowning. The first-aid is to wash the stung area in alcohol and get the patient into hospital and on oxygen if he goes into shock.

Occasionally, the prevailing winds bring thousands of jellyfish into coastal areas, prompting the resorts to post warning notices.

Coral can not only cut, but the **fire coral** can sting and **sea urchins** can cause nasty wounds if stepped on. For safety, always wear goggles when swimming around coral so you can see what not to touch.

Pests: mosquitos. Mosquitos can be a real problem at night in the cheaper non-tourist hotels where there is no netting across the windows, and sometimes not even any glass. Carry some suitable repellent such as Autan, or a net to string up. You can buy net in the Dominican Republic, and it's usually possible to rig it to nails conveniently in the walls, or to wooden roof supports; other people before you have had the same problem.

Sand flies. Sand flies, known as *jejenes*, ('hehenes') can drive you absolutely frantic on some beaches, especially towards sunset. They are tiny black creatures that are scarcely visible but which leave a bite that will itch for days, and if you're not careful you can have a rash of tiny pimples. I find the night after being bitten is even worse than the first night.

Jejenes live mainly on the wilder beaches that have not been cleared of decomposing kelp and undergrowth, but as the sands popular with the tourists are kept clean and sprayed, *jejenes* present little problem. I also find the Atlantic coast is less prone than the Caribbean.

Independent or package?

Package. There are package deals operating from many points in Europe and North America to the Dominican Republic. Charter flights to Puerto Plata, Punta Cana and La Romana airports can bring you to within several hundred yards of your modern, air-conditioned hotel overlooking a sun-soaked, white, palm-fringed beach; failing that you will be met by an air-conditioned coach at the Aeropuerto Las Américas in Santo Domingo, and whisked off to your hotel within a couple of hours of arrival. As the sun is shining at a perfect 25°C all year round, this is a guaranteed way of banishing midwinter gloom.

Your hotel provides everything. There is entertainment in the evenings; there are excursions and expeditions organised to places such as Santo Domingo, Altos de Chavón, and other points of interest. There are sports at your disposal, from horse-riding to most forms of aquatics. The hotel is built along the edge of a beautiful beach, and there are guards to keep the local people off your hallowed sands. The food is of good quality, but not as typical as you would find in the local town. There is a constant supply of electricity and drinkable water as the hotel has its own generator — but some tour operators, with a mind to possible litigation, warn that power and water may be cut off for short periods.

On such a package tour you need never put one foot outside the hotel compound and you can have a fortnight of sheer hedonism — at 1989 prices ranging from £350 to £700 per person; Sunquest was offering ten-day holidays from the States for US$420.

Independent. There are many ways of getting to the Dominican Republic by air independently, especially via Miami or New York. European travellers looking for the cheapest flights should concentrate on Virgin Atlantic's and other airlines' standby fares from Gatwick to Miami or New York — but by definition a standby ticket is bought only hours before departure and is one-way only. *You cannot enter the USA on a one-way ticket unless you have a visa.*

Once in the Dominican Republic you can rent a car or jeep at the airport; if you landed at Santo Domingo you can get a *motoconcho* to the main road, Autopista Las Américas, the Las Américas Highway, and get a *guagua,* a local bus, into the capital. From here you can continue on the low-budget plan, spending less than US$20 a day, everything included. This way you will see the the country as it really is and get to know its people, who are friendly and ready to help.

A variation on the theme would be to intersperse the cheap hotels every now and then with a more expensive one so you can clean up and sleep in a comfortable bed.

Another option for the independent traveller is to contact one of the tour operators such as Prieto Tours in Santo Domingo, Puerto Plata or Santiago, and go on a weekend package to one of the tourist hotels or visit some of the country's scenic attractions.

Dominican Embassies and Consulates.

Some embassies and consulates of the Dominican Republic in other countries:

Canada: Consulate General of the Dominican Republic, 25 Adelaide St East, Toronto, Ontario, ✆(416).364.7231.

Spain: Embajada Dominicana, Paseo de la Castellana 30, Madrid 28048, ✆431.5395.

United Kingdom: Jane Wardener, Honorary Consul for the Dominican Republic, 6 Queen's Mansions, Brook Greeen, London W6 7EB, ✆071.602.1885.

USA: Embassy of the Dominican Republic, 1715 East 22nd St, Washington, DC 2008, ✆(202).332.6280−2.

And some embassies and consulates of other countries in the Dominican Republic:

France: Av George Washington 353, ✆689.2161.
Germany (West): C/ T.J. Mejía 37, ✆565.8812.
Italy: Rodriguez Obijo 4, ✆682.0830.
Netherlands: Leopoldo Navarro, ✆682.3594.
Spain: Av Independencia 1205, ✆533.1424.
Switzerland: José Gabriel García 26, ✆689.4131.
United Kingdom: Av Independencia 506, ✆682.3128.
USA: César Nicolás Penson, ✆682.2171.

Tourist Information Offices in other countries:

Canada: 24 Bellair St, Toronto, Ont MR5 2C8, ✆(416).928.9188–9284.1464 Crescent St, Montreal, Que H3A 2B6, ✆(514).843.3418.

Puerto Rico: Edificio Miramar Plaza, Ponce de Léon 954, Santurce, P.R., ✆(809).725.4774.

Spain: Nuñez de Balboa 37 4to Izq, Madrid 1, ✆(01).431.5354.

USA: 485 Madison Ave, 2nd floor, New York, NY 10022, ✆(212).826.0750.2355 Salzedo St, Suite 305, Coral Gables, Miami, FL 33134, ✆(305).444.4592–3. or dial 800.752.1151 anywhere in the USA.

Tourist Information Offices in the Dominican Republic:

Santo Domingo: Secretaría de Estado de Turismo, (Ministry of Tourism), Avenida George Washington, ✆(809)682.8181. (The staff are efficient and very friendly) Tourist Office, Long Beach, Puerto Plata, at eastern end of the Malecón (I found the staff here to be rather uninformative).

Where to go.

The main tourist areas are, as you would expect, around the best beaches, which in the north are at Puerto Plata, the 'Port of Silver,' and Sosúa; in the south-east at Punta Cana and Bavaro Beach; and on the Caribbean coast at La Romana with its Casa de Campo, 68 miles (110km) east of Santo Domingo. These areas have many good-quality hotels and beaches that offer all that the average sunloving tourist seeks.

Another well-known strand is Boca Chica, Santo Domingo's own beach which is lively, and packed at weekends by partying Dominicans. Tourist hotels have started to rise here as well.

A further area that is developing into a tourist complex is Juan Dolio, just to the west of San Pedro de Macoris, but the region lacks top-quality beaches. The superb sands between Sosúa and Samaná are slowly attracting foreign visitors, who find Samaná itself to be a jewel of a town.

The entire east coast, with its 43 miles (70km) of sands from Bavaro Beach to Sabana de la Mar, is totally unspoilt and without any tourist services at all. And if you want to plant your feet in near virgin sands, come to the beautiful coastline which runs south from Barahona — but again, there's no tourist infrastructure.

Santo Domingo. The capital city itself is generally a hot and noisy metropolis that has some very poor districts yet can offer some pleasant corners. It's not the main attraction of the republic, but is useful for shopping and any other business. It has its quota of expensive hotels, restaurants and nightclubs, but its lack of a beach is a major disadvantage for the average tourist.

The interior of the island is unspoiled and extremely beautiful; the mountains are refreshing, and towns such as Jarabacoa and Constanza are well worth a visit, especially to see the waterfalls and walk in the mountains.

When to go.

The tourist season is year-round, thanks to the country's tropical climate. North Americans, whose winter playground is limited to Florida and the Caribbean, come south in large numbers, making December through April the Dominican Republic's high season.

North Europeans have other options for midwinter escapes, so they head for the republic between April and November, taking advantage of low season prices. The risk is, of course, that a surge of summer visitors will send all prices to high season levels.

Charter flights don't operate from Europe during winter, so any intending visitor who wants to avoid the excesses of summer must either travel on scheduled services or travel via the United States or other Caribbean islands; see Chap 6.

What to take.

Travellers should not think they are going to the equivalent of darkest Africa when heading for the Dominican Republic. Most things are easily available here, and more often than not they're no more expensive than in Europe; they're often cheaper. For example, all articles for personal hygiene such as soap, shampoo, toothpaste and toilet paper are available everywhere. Buy your lightweight tropical shirts, your Bermuda shorts and sun hat when you arrive.

But there are exceptions: film is more expensive than in Britain or the USA, books tend to be scarce and quite expensive, good maps of the island are not available (see 'maps' in Chapter 11), and medicines, sun creams and insect repellents are costly.

Medicines. Bring a first-aid kit with your selection from diarrhoea remedies, creams for skin infections and insect bites, antiseptic cream, adhesive plaster, a small bottle of disinfectant for cuts and scratches and, if you have problems with your ears when swimming, bring some appropriate drops. You might also fancy adding a few Aspirins.

If you plan to walk for several days in a National Park you'll need purifying tablets for the water you collect from the streams, and lots of insect repellant and insect bite cream.

Condoms are available at chemists — look for *farmacia* signs — throughout the country.

Clothing. Lightweight clothing made from cotton is the most practical and comfortable; tee-shirts and jeans, offset by training shoes, and supplemented by a decent set of clothes for going out in the evenings — many *discotecas* won't accept you in scruffy jeans.

For the beach, bring your own goggles, snorkel and fins, and your sunglasses. The law forbids women to go topless in public places, which include the beaches, but this rule is being ignored more each year.

You will need a sweater and a sleeping-bag only if you're planning to stay in the *Cordillera Central,* the central mountains, overnight or in winter, and a waterproof overgarment is useful in the highlands for when you're caught in a sudden downpour, or if you're on a motor-cycle.

Motor-cycling extras. Scarcely any of the Dominicans wear crash-helmets, so bring your own — with a good visor as protection from insects at dusk and the occasional shower. Add some elastic straps for attaching your rucksack to the pannier.

Travelling rough. As the cheaper hotels don't have electricity available all night, bring a small torch for auxiliary lighting — and put it in a convenient spot when you go to bed! Don't bother with a sleeping-bag as the heat will be intolerable, but for those poorer hotels whose sheets are of doubtful cleanliness, I advise you take your own cotton sheet. These cheaper hotels don't have mosquito nets either, but they certainly have mosquitos. You can carry your own net which you can improvise above the bed — reasonable nets are available in the country for around RD$25 (US$4, £2.50) — but you'll be adding to your luggage and making your sleeping conditions hotter and stuffier.

Carry your money, passport, tickets and other valuables securely, either in a money belt (uncomfortable in a hot climate and you'll need to have everything in little plastic bags) or in a purse hanging from your neck.

Photography. The Dominican Republic is a photographer's para-dise, with beautiful and strong colours enhanced — most of the time — by bright sunshine and perfect weather. The countryside is truly impressive and its inhabitants have no objections whatever to being

Suspicion soon turns to a broad smile on children's faces whenever they see a camera.

photographed. Kodak film is almost the only make on the local market and is available everywhere, but be careful about buying it in small shops lacking proper storage facilities. You want other brands? Then bring them with you.

Gifts. The Dominicans are poor people, and know it, so don't be surprised or offended if you're asked for money. The problem is that in the long term, giving money is not a good policy unless it's in payment for services, information, or out of compassion for somebody down on his luck, but there are times when it's the most prudent act, particularly if you have a persistent hassler.

When begging children become too demanding it's probably better to give them a stick of chewing gum, *un chicle,* rather than money, as the latter will only serve to confirm them as beggars.

In the countryside you will often meet genuine warmth and hospitality among the adult population and you will want to offer them a token gift. One ideal offering is a photograph of the family; if you don't have the film processed in the country you can always post it back, provided you ask for the address. Another solution is to go equipped with small items for their children, such as pencils, pencil sharpeners, and notepads; even the adults like to receive small gifts such as cigarette lighters, with foreign writing on them.

The larger towns have orphanages run by *las monjas,* the nuns; these are charities and if you cared to give some money you would be certain that it reached the people for whom you intended it.

Disabled. &

The Dominican Republic is not equipped in any way for disabled people. There are no toilets — restrooms — for people in wheelchairs, nor is there any consideration made for them, and as the streets are full of pot-holes, progress would be hazardous. There are very few wheelchairs in the country — but a disabled visitor could certainly expect to find the locals ready to help in any way possible.

Tour operators.

Tour operators offering package holidays to the Dominican Republic include:

from Canada: Adventure Tours (Ont), Albatours (Ont), Conquest Tours (Ont), Fiesta Holidays (Ont), Regent Holidays (Ont), Mirabelle Tours (Ont), Solvac Tours (Que), Sunquest (Ont), Treasure Tours (Que).

from Germany (West): Air Marin, Airtours International, Turistik Union International (T.U.I.).

from Sweden: Columbus Resort.

from Switzerland: Hotel Plan, Carib Tours.

from the UK: Airtours, Cosmos, Intasun, Island Sun, Thomson, Turavia.

from the USA (New York and region except where stated): Adventure Tours (Dallas), A.O.T. Tours, Beraldi Tours (Miami), Caribbean Holidays, Cavalcade Tours, Fantastic Tours (Dallas), Flyfare, G.I.T. Tours (Miami), Gogo Tours, Hotelink (Tourlink), Liberty Travel, Marazul Tours, Mena International Travel (Miami), Metropolis Tours (Miami), Sunburst Holidays, Trails Travel & Tourism (Miami), Travel Consolidators, Travel Impressions, Travelot, Turavia International (Miami).

In addition, there are many charter flights from Italy.

Un chin is the Dominican for 'a little,' and you will hear it everywhere.

3: MONEY MATTERS
And cost of living

THE CURRENCY OF THE DOMINICAN REPUBLIC is the peso, abbreviated to RD$ — which means that throughout this book the United States dollar and the Dominican peso are shown as US$ and RD$ respectively. *Peso* means 'weight,' among other things, but the currency has suffered a bad attack of inflation, taking it from the official rate of RD$1.35 to the pound in 1984 to RD$10 to the pound (RD$6.5 to the US dollar) in 1989; during that time the unofficial rate gradually crept up, forcing an official devaluation, but since 14 July 1988 the government has tried, not with complete success, to hold the currency at RD$6.28 to US$1.

Bring dollars. The mighty US dollar is the Dominicans' guardian angel, and is the currency that tourists should bring, either in travellers' cheques (travelers' checks) or cash. Dominicans are not familiar with European monies, although the Banco Central in Santo Domingo and the exchange offices at the Banco de Reservas at Las Américas Airport will change European and Canadian money.

Despite that, the peso is the only currency acceptable in the Dominican Republic. You cannot pay legally for anything in the country in any foreign currency, which means that almost your first task on arrival is to buy your pesos — and the only place you can do it is in a bank or a change bureau: look for the sign *banco de cambio* at the major hotels. It's worth noting that all money-changing outlets are controlled by a government department known as the *Junta Monetaria*. You cannot buy pesos outside the country as the currency is 'soft,' not traded on world markets — and it's not even negotiable in neighbouring Haiti.

Restrictions and reconversion. There is no restriction on the amount of money you may bring into the republic, but you may take out no more than the equivalent of US$5,000, in cash or travellers' cheques. As you trade your dollars for pesos you'll be given receipts which you must keep to show at the Banco de Reservas, with your passport, when you leave; you can then reconvert up to a maximum of 30% of the pesos you've bought. Note that banks in the country have the right to buy US dollars, but not to sell them.

The currency. The peso is divided into 100 centavos. There are coins valued at 1, 5, 10, 25 and 50 centavos, and bank notes − bills − in these denominations: RD$1, yellow-brown; RD$5, red; RD$10, dark green; RD$20, brown; RD$50, purple, RD$100, orange, RD$500, pale turquoise; RD$1,000, magenta. The last two are virtually useless in rural areas and indeed in most towns, as few people have enough money to change them.

Black market. It's not advisable to change money on the streets. In Conde St in the capital you may be approached by self-styled money-changers who are really nothing more than tricksters, and you will lose every time; as it is, the presumed gain is marginal compared with the official exchange rate at the bank. Most of these men must have been magicians before they discovered they could make more money out of fooling the tourists, but luckily they stick closely to their territory.

Credit cards. 'Plastic' is well-established in the Dominican Republic; probably more so than in some European countries. The most common cards in use are Visa, American Express, and Mastercard, which also takes Britain's Access cards; Diners Club is not so popular. You can pay by plastic in restaurants, hotels, galleries, travel agencies and shops, wherever there is a hint of tourism to be detected. Obviously, a credit card would be a novelty in a village corner shop.

It's easy to buy money in banks with your credit card, but you must

When were the Romans in the Dominican Republic? This amphitheatre is in Altos de Chavón.

expect to pay around 2% for the transaction. You will, of course, only get pesos, and you must keep your receipt.

Personal cheques. You cannot cash personal cheques in the country, even with the support of a guarantee card.

Banking hours. Banks are open Mon-Fri 0830-1730 and, for changing money *only*, on Sat 0800-1200.

Cost of living.

The cost of living is continually rising because of inflation and the effects of the tourist industry, but prices of the basic produce of the land are still less than in North America or northern Europe. Imported goods are expensive, yet readily available.

Prices vary from one supermarket to another, making it worth looking around to decide which is the cheapest store. The following prices are an average for the summer of 1989, with the first figure, in **bold type,** being in pesos, the second in US dollars.

Aspirins, pack of 4 .... **$1.20,** 20¢, *12p.*
Batteries, 2 Duracell AA **$15.85,** $2.50, *£1.60*
Beer, Bohemia, 6 x 355ml bottles **$14.10,** $2.25, *£1.40*
–, Heineken, 6 x 280ml bottles **$19.99,** $3.20, *£2*
Bread, French loaf .... **$2.50,** 40¢, *25p*
Butter, Rica, 1lb **$10,** $1.60, *£1*
Cheese, Philadelphia, 8oz **$18.95,** $3, *£1.90*
Cigarettes, 20 Marlboro .... **$3,** 47¢, *30p*
–, 20 Nacional .... **$2.50,** 40¢, *25p*
Cigars, box 25 Aurora Sublime **$138,** $22, *£13.80*
–,– 25 – Petit Corona **$77.99,** $12.40, *£7.80*
–,– 25 – La Habanera Especial **$50.49,** $8, *£5*
Coca Cola, bottle .... **$1.75,** 28¢, *18p*
Coffee, Sto Domingo, 1lb **$6.89,** $1.10, *69p*
–, Nescafé, 40z **$38.89,** $6.20, *39p*
Cooking oil, corn, 120fl.oz **$43.95,** $7, *£4.40*
– –, olive, 628gm, ... **$24.49,** $3.90, *£2.50*
Eggs, doz .... **$5.40,** 86¢, *54p*
Fruit, each: avocado .... **$2,** 32¢, *20p*
– –, banana .... **40c,** 6¢, *4p*
– –, grapefruit .... **50c,** 8¢, *5p*
– –, mango .... **$1,** 16¢, *10p*
– –, melon .... **$3,** 56¢, *30p*
Gin, Gordons, 75cl **$92.75,** $14.77, *£9.27*
–, Bermudez, 75cl **$13.95,** $2.22, *£1.40*
Honey, big pot **$8.50,** $1.35, *85p*
Kellogg's corn flakes, 1lb **$18.25,** $2.90, *£1.82*

Milk, La Vaquita, 946ml .... **$3**, 47¢, *30p*
—, Nestlé condensed, 405gm .... **$4.99**, 80¢, *49p*
Mineral water, Crystal, 1 gal **$6.25**, $1, *62p*
Rum, Macorix, 8yr old **$15.50**, $2.47, *£1.55*
—, Bermudez Dorado, 40° **$13.25**, $2.10, *£1.32*
Shampoo, local, 300cc **$9.99**, $1.60, *£1*
—, Johnson's, 3½oz **$7.75**, $1.23, *77p*
Tea bags, 100 Lipton **$34.95**, $5.56, *£3.50*
Tomato ketchup, Victoria, 14oz .... **$4.50**, 71¢, *45p*
Vinegar, 450cc .... **$2.99**, 47¢, *29p*
Vodka, Wyborowa, 75cl, 40° **$55.95**, $8.90, *£5.60*
—, Stolichnaya, 75cl, 40° **$89.90**, $14.30, *£9*
Whisky, J&B, 75cl **$84.95**, $13.52, *£8.50*
—, J Walker Red Label, 75cl **$84.95**, $13.52, *£8.50*
—, — — Black Label, 75cl **$139.95**, 22.30, *£14*
Wine, Rioja, Spanish, 70cl **$29.50**, $4.70, *£2.95*
—, Gato Negro, Chilean, 70cl **$32.95**, $5.25, *£3.30*
—, Bordeaux, French, 75cl **$45.95**, $7.30, *£4.60*

Bus fare by *guagua*, La Romana — Sto Domingo (110km) ....RD$6
Basic wages:
Labourer in Free Zone factory, month .. ..RD$500, US$80, £50
Policeman, month ....RD$500, US$80, £50
Teacher, month ....RD$600, US$96, £60
Secretary, month .... RD$900, US$144, £90

Founding father Duarte still appears on the local currency.

4: LANGUAGE

Spanish, English, Patois

THE OFFICIAL LANGUAGE of the Dominican Republic is Spanish, but it is not the Castilian — the *Castillano* — of Madrid. As with all the Spanish-speaking lands of the Americas, it has taken the dialects of Spain's provinces of Extremadura and Andalucía, from where its conquerors and settlers came.

Dominican Spanish. The republic has also developed its own distinctive accent and vocabulary, which at times can mean that Spaniards and Dominicans have difficulties in understanding each other. In addition, Dominican Spanish has held on to many words from 16th-cent Spanish which have long since vanished from Castillano, such as *platicar*, 'to speak,' instead of *hablar; desbaratar* instead of *romper*, 'to break' — and *vosotros*, the familiar plural form of 'you,' does not exist.

Loan words. The Dominicans have absorbed many American words that are unknown in European Spanish. *Chequear* is 'to check', *un cluche* is 'a clutch,' *un par de zapatos brown* is 'a pair of brown shoes,' and *bye bye* has replaced *adios.*

Dominican Spanish has many Taíno Indian words, some of which have carried on into English almost without change. Did you, for instance, know that these words were Taíno: *barbacoa*, 'barbecue;' *canoa*, 'canoe;' *caribe*, the Caribbean; *hamaca*, 'hammock;' *huracán*, 'hurricane;' and the startlingly obvious ones; *iguana, maiz, tabaco* and *yuca.*

Another problem facing the visitor who has learned Castilian Spanish is that some Dominican Spanish words have changed their meaning, as 'pavement' has on its journey across the Atlantic. *Una vaina* is 'a thing,' not 'a pod,' and *guapo (guapa)* means 'angry' instead of 'pretty.'

The lesson is obvious. If you learned Spanish in Europe, don't be alarmed or disappointed if it seems that the Dominicans aren't speaking the same language, or if they stare blankly at you when you've said something in perfectly correct *Castillano*. In particular, don't get upset when you ask for 'two beers,' *dos cervezas* in Madrid, but find yourself served with twelve beers in Santo Domingo. The

Andaluz dialect usually drops the final letter, particularly when it's 's,' hence the Dominican dialect does so as well. 'Twelve,' *doce,* comes out as 'dos,' which is 'two' — while the real two, *dos,* comes out as 'dô.' Just make sure you hold up the correct number of fingers when you're ordering!

In summary: a knowledge of Spanish — *any* Spanish — is a great help in the Dominican Republic, particularly if you intend travelling in the remoter parts of the country, but total ignorance of the language is no barrier to enjoying a holiday in this friendly land.

English. Most Dominicans, particularly the youngsters, have at least a smattering of English and are forever looking for a chance to practise it and show off their skills. I've been in restaurants where I've had verbal battles with waiters to whom I insisted on speaking Spanish, while they insisted on replying in English.

At other times, particularly in the countryside, you may meet somebody such as a tyre repair man, a *gomero,* or a mechanic (*mecánico*) who will refuse to believe that any foreigner, *gringo,* can speak Spanish, and even though you address him fluently in that language he'll answer you as if he's talking to an idiot, pausing for at least a second between words and using verbs in the infinitive instead of conjugating them. He may be trying to help, as he sees it, but at times this 'easy Spanish' is incomprehensible.

Throughout the tourist areas you'll have no language troubles even if you speak not a word of anything but English, which is now an unofficial second language in the Dominican Republic, mainly for economic reasons. The Dominican who has some command of English has a better chance of employment in the higher-paid tourist industry and in the factories in the Free Zones, and English is near-vital if his ambition is to find work in the United States.

As a result, Dominicans have no hesitation in talking to you in English, and I find that *inglés* is understood deeper into the back country here than it is in Spain.

Other languages. In the bigger tourist hotels most staff also speak some Italian and French as well as English, but few know any German — although economic incentives urge Dominicans to learn another language if sufficient visitors have it as their mother tongue.

Patois. It may come as a surprise to learn that some of the people you see working in the country are not even conversant in Dominican Spanish. The vast majority of the cane-cutters, and the roadbuilding labourers in the cities, come from Haiti as an economic necessity, and are temporary residents in the Dominican Republic. They learn just enough Spanish to get by, but among themselves they speak their patois, a mixture of French, English, Spanish, and Yoruba, their ancestral tongue from Africa.

Your Dominican-Spanish Vocabulary

English	Dominican-Spanish	Pronunciation
Motoring:		
car	carro	
gas (petrol)	gasolina	
full (e.g., tank)	lleno	Yayno
two-stroke oil	aceite de dos tiempos	
diesel (gas-oil)	gas-oil	
tyre (tire)	goma	
air (for tyre)	aire	ayree
one-way street	una via	
roundabout	rotonda	
traffic lights	semáforo	se-*maff*-oro
breakdown	avería	aver-*ee*-ah
In town:		
post office	correos	co-*ray*-os
stamps	sellos	selyos
envelope	sobre	sobray
Canada	Canadá	(stress the á)
England	Inglaterra	
Germany	Alemania	
Ireland	Irlandia	
Scotland	Escocia	
United States	Estados Unidos	es-*ta*-dos un-*ee*-dos
(note that 'USA' is written 'EE.UU.')		
shop	tienda	
open	abierto	
closed	cerrado	
how much is it?	¿Cuánto es?	
too much	demasiado	
small change (money)	menudo	
where is...?	¿dónde está...?	don-des-*tah*?
when?	¿Cuándo?	
In the hotel:		
double room	habitación doble	— — doblay
bed	cama	
hot water	agua caliente	awa — —
fan	abanico	
mosquito net	mosquitero	
restaurant	restaurante	resto-rantay
breakfast	desayuno	
midday meal	comida	
evening meal	cena	say-na
waiter	camarero	

English	Dominican-Spanish	Pronunciation
Out and about:		
beach	playa	
sand	arena	ar-*ay*-na
sea	mar	
rain	lluvia	you-*vee*-ah
sun	sol	
quiet (quiet spot)	tranquilo	
noise	bulla	booya
near	cerca	
far	retirado *or* lejos	*le*-hoss
on the left	a la izquierda	− − is-*care*-da
on the right	a la derecha	
straight ahead	derecho	

(note the confusing similarity of the last two)

Abbreviations used in the Dominican Republic

Abbreviation	Complete word	English meaning
Apto.	Apartamento	Apartment
Av.	Avenida	Avenue
C/	Cálle	Street
Esq.	Esquina	Corner
Gral.	General	General (in street names)
#	Número	Number
Pto. Pta.	Puerto Plata	
R.D.	República Dominicana	
Sto. Dgo.	Santo Domingo.	

The Taino Indians called the Dominican Republic *Quisqueya*,
which is now the name of a popular beer.

5: RELIGION

Voodoo and Catholicism

THE MAIN RELIGION IS CATHOLICISM, but tourists usually find the hint of voodoo to be much more intriguing. Voodoo in its purest sense is not intended for the tourist and is practised secretly in the hills far from prying eyes. Its origins are African and involve ancestor worship, but one of the more dramatic events in a voodoo ritual occurs when a participant gives control of his or her body to a spirit from the dead, presumably that of an ancestor; this is the state of trance in which the possessed person's voice and manner may change radically.

As a person may be taken over by a spirit of the opposite sex, some sceptics and critics point out that a voodoo ceremony may provide a good excuse for repressed homosexuals to express their urges.

Black magic. Voodoo is often confused with black magic, and there is indeed a hint of the more sinister side of occultism in beliefs and practises such as animism, which claims that a living person's soul or spirit can be lodged in an inanimate object — and so leads us to the malevolent practise of sticking pins into a doll-like effigy in order to inflict pain on the person represented.

Voodoo exponents believe in the ability of a living body to change into another creature, such as a wolf, and to raise the bodies of the dead: hence the legends of the werewolf and the zombie so popular with the makers of horror-movies.

Voodoo gods. Strictly speaking, voodoo is more often associated with Haiti whose gods — *loas* — differ considerably from those in the Dominican Republic where you find loas with names such as Papa Legba, El Barón del Cementerio, Papa Candelo and La Baronesa Briggette.

Seeing voodoo? My feeling is that the tourist who wants to see voodoo should do so from the safety and comfort of an excursion organised by a local tour company as there really is no such thing as a passive observer in a voodoo or a black magic rite. If this really is for you, buy a place on the Bavaro Beach Hotel's journey up the Chavón River to a Haitian cane-cutter's village — known as a *batey* — where the residents put on a voodoo show of sorts. Or try in Santo

Ready for a day's work with the cattle. The saddle is home-made from straw and sacking.

Domingo itself, where the International Caribbean Club, ✆543.7249, advertises a voodoo show on Wednesday nights starting at 2130hrs; it's at km 13.5 on Autopista Duarte. This sort of show presents the best opportunity for photography, though you may be expected to pay for each shot.

During Easter there are many voodoo festivals throughout the country, the best-known being in the *bateyes* (an unfortunate plural; don't think of it as 'bat-eyes') where the gagá dancers send themselves into a trance: for a fuller explanation see 'festivals' in Chapter 11.

Then there is *El Baile de Palos*, the 'cane dance' of El Seibo and, in May, a series of dances in the rural villages and the cane-growing areas, with performers dressed in bright costumes in their desire to attract particular loas.The dances frequently spill out onto the roads, and travellers may have to pay a small toll to get past.

After you've seen several performances such as these you will have an insight into yet another aspect of Dominican culture – the language of the drum, as there are more than 200 rhythms of drumbeat used in the country.

Evil eye. Dominicans are extremely superstitious and genuinely believe in the evil eye, *mal de ojo*, and the power of the curse. If, for example, a baby is born with its legs back to front, called *ciguapa*, people suspect it's the result of a curse rather than a biological defect. Every town in the country has its own well-known witches and worlocks – *brujas* and *brujos* – whom the people consult.

Virgin of Altagracia. Country people have mixed voodoo and Catholicism to the extent that one could almost say a new religion has been created. An exciting demonstration of this mixture can be seen annually on 21 January in the homage paid by devotees to the cult of the Virgin of Altagracia, the patron saint of the Dominican Republic. People walk from all parts of the country, some spending up to five days on the road and carrying banners and images, pausing at little roadside shrines in the villages to sing to the Virgin, but all congregating at the Basílica (Cathedral) of Higuey in the south-east for a general mixture of prayers and festivity.

And on 16 August, which is also a special day in the Dominican Republic, singing cowboys round up cattle and send them as gifts to the Virgin at Higuey.

When I asked one old man why he was doing the January pilgrimage he told me it was to appease God and to protect the country from earthquakes and hurricanes. The terrible landslide of September 1987 which destroyed the Colombian town of Villa Tina by Medellín was, he said, punishment for the Colombians because they hadn't paid their respects to the Virgin of Altagracia!

The Catholic Church. Roman Catholicism is the leading orthodox religion in the country, with its followers mainly coming from the upper classes. The Church has an archdiocese in Santo Domingo – *La Primada de América,* the 'first in America' – established in 1511; the present archbishop is Nicolás de Jesús López Rodriguez. The country is divided into eight sees.

Other sects. The working class and the poor are more attracted to the evangelical churches, which range from the Seventh Day Adventists to the Temple of Jehovah. The protestant section of the community has always been strong, originally nurtured by the slaves shipped over from Protestant Jamaica and in later years reflecting the strong influence from the United States. On any Sunday you can see the white-shirted devotees singing and clapping in their church services, which I feel is much more in tune with the easy-going Dominican mentality than is the more formal Catholic ceremonial.

The Seventh Day Adventists have a University in Bonao and give a free education to anybody who wants to become a preacher for the sect, a wonderful incentive to the poor.

6: GETTING TO THE DOMINICAN REPUBLIC

By air only

THE 'BEST KEPT SECRET IN THE CARIBBEAN' is now easily accessible by scheduled and charter airlines from North America and Europe; in fact, the Dominican Republic boasts a dazzling array of airlines operating scheduled services from its international airports, the *Aeropuerto Internacional de las Américas*, 25 minutes from Santo Domingo, and the *Aeropuerto Internacional La Unión*, 20 minutes from Puerto Plata and 15 from Sosúa. Most airlines offer two flights weekly except for the routes to Miami, New York, and San Juan in Puerto Rico, which have daily services.

Scheduled services

From North America. The US or Canadian citizen has no problem in getting a direct flight to the Dominican Republic. From **New York** American Airlines (AA) has 3 flights daily to Santo Domingo, Eastern (EA) has 1 or 2, Pan Am (PA) and Dominicana de Aviación (DO) each has 1. In addition, AA, DO and Continental each has a daily flight to Puerto Plata.

From **Miami.** AA has up to 5 daily flights to Santo Domingo, EA has 2, and PA and DO each has 1. In addition, AA has one daily flight to Puerto Plata and DO and PA each has 3 weekly flights.

From Canada. Air Canada has a total of 3 flights a week from Toronto and Montreal to Puerto Plata.

From Europe. There are no direct scheduled services from Britain but from Paris there are two a week, from Madrid five, and from Frankfurt three (via Puerto Rico). In addition, ALM (Antillean Airlines, the Caribbean subsidiary of KLM) operates from Amsterdam via Curaçao, and there are plans for Bal Air, a subsidiary of Swissair, to open a direct service from Zürich.

These fares are, of course, expensive; at the time of writing the cheapest return fare from Frankfurt – low season economy – is US$946.

Charter flights

The independent European traveller looking for the cheapest flight has the option of buying a flight-only package from one of the major tour operators during the summer season, or going via the USA. Among the British charter airlines operating direct flights are Novair and Air 2000, but you must book via your travel agent, or through the Air Traffic Advisory Bureau, ✆London 071.636.5000, Manchester 061.832.2000, or Birmingham 021.783.2000.

The American option is to take a standby to Miami (at the time of writing Virgin Airlines asks something less than £100 each way) and then *either* a scheduled to Santo Domingo — the cheapest return fare on this leg is US$134 with DO — *or* to Haiti. In this instance you should fly on to Santo Domingo rather than consider going overland as the frontier is frequently closed for short periods with no apparent reason, and when it's open the formalities are a mess. *Note that the Miami option is available only if you have a US visa.*

From the Caribbean. You can fly in from San Juan, **Puerto Rico**; AA has 4 flights daily, DO has 2, EA has 1, and Lufthansa has 2 weekly. From **Haiti**'s Port au Prince you can fly with PA to Santo Domingo 4 times weekly, or daily on a Haitian line.

How do you get to Haiti? One option is to come in from Miami with PA, for 400 goude return, which converts at £50.

The Turks & Caicos National Airline flies in twice weekly from Grand Turk to Puerto Plata in a De Havilland-7. Now *that* would make an interesting route in via Miami!

Miscellaneous arrivals. Aeropostal flies in from Curaçao; Air Aruba flies in from there and from the island of Aruba; Air France comes in from Guadeloupe; ALM from San Martin; Avianca flies in from Colombia; Copa from Panama; DO from Venezuela; Emily Tours from Cuba; Iberia from Costa Rica, Guatemala, Nicaragua and Pánama; and Viasa from Venezuela and Curaçao.

The airlines listed below have these offices in Santo Domingo:

Aeropostal, Punta Caucedo, ✆549.0010.

Air Canada, Av J.F. Kennedy (corner site), ✆567.2236–7.

Air France, Av. G Washington 101, ✆686.8419.

ALM, Leopoldo Navarro 28, ✆687.4594.

American Airlines, El Conde 401, ✆686.7050.

Avianca, Roberto Pastoriza 401, ✆562.1797.

Continental Airlines, (city:) ✆686.7410, 7415; Puerto Plata Airport, ✆586.0286, 0309.

Copa, Av Tiradentes 10a, ✆562.6815, 36584.

Cubana de Aviación, (of which Emily Tours is the charter side), San Fransisco de Macoris 58, ✆682.9000, 688.1923.

Dominicana de Aviación, Av W Churchill, ✆532.8511.

Eastern Airlines, El Conde 403, ✆686.9191.

Iberian Airlines, El Conde 401, ✆685.7171, 689.9176. (The above two phone numbers are correct; there's little logic in the Dominican

Dance floors at Boca de Yuma have a splendid view out to sea.

phone system.)

    Lufthansa, Av G Washington 353, ✆689.9625.
    Pan American, Av 27 de Febrero, ✆541.8000, 566.4742.
    Varig, Plaza Lincoln, ✆566.1102.
    Viasa, Leopoldo Navarro 28, ✆687.2688.

The Airports

    Las Américas International, ✆549.0421 and 549.0400, the Dominican Republic's main airport, is 19 miles (30km) from the capital, Santo Domingo, hence its airport denominator, SDQ; watch for these letters on your baggage check-in labels and your luggage shouldn't go astray.

    Customs. The customs formalities are usually straightforward, with your incoming baggage warranting no more than a cursory inspection. You are allowed to import a litre of spirits, 200 cigarettes, and gifts up to a value of US$100. The airport is constantly being improved, which means that on a good day you can pass through fairly quickly, but on a bad day you can expect a fair degree of disorganisation. The worst time is just before Christmas when all the 'Dominican Yorks' (Dominicans with US residence permits who usually live in New York) are coming home for the holiday.

Services. Codetel has an excellent international telephone exchange, and there are phones for local calls; several exchange banks compete for business, but the restaurant does not operate a 24-hour service. There are four sets of restrooms (toilets) around the airport, but none in the baggage-reclaim area.

Luggage warning. Baggage may be pilfered on its way through to the carousel, with shoes being the usual target. The answer is to lock your bag; if it doesn't have a fitted lock, put a light chain and padlock around it.

Transport. There is no public transport from the airport. While package tourists are collected by coach, everybody else has to make his or her own way, the most common being by taxi from the ranks in front of the customs hall.

These taxis are large Chevrolets which have seen far better times and they operate with set charges to each destination, but this is no deterrent to the driver trying to ask for more. The fare is RD$225 (US$35) to Santo Domingo and RD$175 (US$28) to La Romana.

You have the option of taking a *carro público* from the airport down to Las Américas Highway for a few pesos and then waving down a *guagua,* either to Santo Domingo or La Romana; there are also eight auto-rental agencies just beyond the customs hall (see the next chapter for public transport and car rentals).

Exit tax. *Note that there is an airport tax charged on every departing tourist. It is currently US$10: don't forget to keep this money available.*

Duty-free shops. A dozen or so duty-free shops sell the usual range of items, but accept only US dollars; change all your Dominican money before you go through immigration control.

Other airports. Puerto Plata Airport (✆586.0310 and 586.0219) is smaller than Las Américas but handles a few international scheduled and charter flights; it is roughly midway between Puerto Plata and Sosúa, with the designator POP. La Romana Airport, LRM, cannot take large airliners but has links with San Juan using smaller machines. In the extreme east, Punta Cana, PUJ, has scheduled links only with Puerto Rico.

Sea arrival.

There is no longer any scheduled service to or from the Dominican Republic by sea, as a counter to the number of stowaways who have made their way to Europe and the USA as illegal immigrants. Even the once-regular car ferry from San Pedro de Macoris to San Juan, Puerto Rico, has been withdrawn from service. You will normally arrive in the country by sea only if you come on a luxury cruise or if you sail your own yacht.

7: TRAVELLING IN THE DOMINICAN REPUBLIC

Public transport and auto rental

THE INDEPENDENT TRAVELLER will have no difficulty in getting around the Dominican Republic; the package tourist can either join in the scramble aboard public transport and have a glimpse at what life is really like for the poorer people of this world, or go for the soft option of taking an organised excursion in air-conditioned comfort.

Throughout the country, even in the remotest mountain village, there is some sort of public transport, be it a *guagua*, a minibus; a *camioneta*, literally a 'little lorry' but in effect a pick-up truck; or a *motoconcho*, the pillion on a Honda 50cc motor-cycle.

Expensive cars. Cars and motor-cycles cost up to two and a half times as much in the Dominican Republic as they do in the USA, where the standard of living is far higher, with the result that few Dominicans can afford their own transport. They are therefore forced to rely on small companies or private individuals who make their living from getting the greatest possible use out of the available transport − without charging tariffs that the locals couldn't afford to pay.

Hitch-hiking. Despite such a demand for transport, hitch-hiking is not common, and the relatively-affluent visitor should not expect to impose on the poorer native population.

Railways. All the transport companies are privately owned; there is no government-financed system. Nor are there any passenger railways; the tracks you see are for trains carrying cane from the fields to the sugar-mills.

PUBLIC TRANSPORT:
Inter-city buses.

The largest and most comfortable buses linking the major towns are operated by Caribe Tours and Metro Buses, and are air-conditioned, fast and efficient, comparable with the tourist coach of Europe or the USA. They are more expensive than the guaguas.

METRO BUSES

Metro Buses operates from offices at the junction of Av Winston Churchill and Hatuey, in Santo Domingo, ∅566.6587, −6590. For seat reservations − strongly recommended − ∅586.3736 in Puerto Plata; ∅582.9111 in Santiago; ∅584.2259 in Nagua.

Daily departures from SANTO DOMINGO to:				Daily returns to SANTO DOMINGO from:			
SANTIAGO							
0700	0730	1000	1100	0700	0800	1000	1245
1330	1500	1600	1730	1500	1630	1715	1800
1830				1930			
PUERTO PLATA							
0730	1100	1600	1830	0700	1130	1500★	1600
1830				★ operates Sunday only.			
NAGUA							
0730	1530			0700	1400		
SAN FRANSISCO de MACORIS							
0730	1530			0800	1500		
CASTILLO							
0730	1530			0730	1430		
LA VEGA							
0730	1600			0730	1600		
MOCA							
0730	1600			0700	1530		

OTHER BUS COMPANIES

Terra Buses operates from offices at 60 Cotubanama in Plaza Criolla, Sto Domingo, ✆565.2333. It runs lighter schedules. **Expresos Mota Saad** of 11 Av Independencia, Sto Domingo, ✆688.7775, connects the capital with Santiago cheaply. **Caribe Tours,** with offices in the capital at the corner of Av 27 de Febrero and Leopoldo Navarro, ✆687.3171, operates daily to Barahona, Bonao, Cabrera, Dajabon, Jarabacoa, La Vega, Monte Cristi, Nagua, Río San Juan, Salcedo, Sánchez, Samaná, San Fransisco, and Villa Vasquez.

Guaguas.

Minibuses known as *guaguas,* pronounced 'gwa-gwa,' are cheaper than the Metro-style buses and serve the entire country apart from the very remote areas. Each guagua's condition depends on its owner; if he is a *tacaño* — a tight-fisted person — then the vehicle will be overcrowded and badly maintained, similar to the 'bush taxi' in remoter parts of Africa.

Squeezing six passengers into five seats is a favourite trick of the guagua owners, providing an endless source of lively discussion throughout the trip. But you might be lucky. Your guagua might be brand new, clean, with all its windows in place, and you may have a seat all to yourself. It's the will of *Dios,* as every Dominican knows, and if Dios has played you a rough hand for your particular journey, just shrug your shoulders and tell yourself "Así son las cosas" — that's life. You are henceforth a seasoned Dominican traveller!

Guagua stations. Guagua stations are normally located on the outskirts of the bigger towns, but this doesn't present any problem as there is constant service of guaguas ferrying people from the town centre — free of charge to the public but financed by the guagua companies themselves. In other towns your guagua may operate directly from a convenient spot in the centre.

Travelling tips. If you're travelling only a short distance by guagua, stay close to the exit or you may be carried beyond your destination; it's probably wiser to avoid the rear seats altogether if possible, as they're not called *la cocina,* 'the kitchen,' for fun. I recommend you try for a seat near the window from where you can get an occasional refreshing blast of cooler air.

Guagua owners are reluctant to accept luggage, and for some reason I've yet to discover they haven't thought about fitting roof racks to their vehicles. You'll have to argue with your guagua driver to induce him to allow you aboard with your rucksack, and you should be prepared to pay for it as if it's another passenger: it may effectively deprive somebody else of a place on the minibus.

Fares. Fares are, in any event, very low: you can travel the 70 miles (110km) from Santo Domingo to La Romana for RD$6 (US$1, 60p). Try to have the correct fare ready, and avoid paying in large-denomination bills — and don't worry if you don't get your change straight away; the young man in charge of collecting the fares normally takes all the money before he gives out the change.

Cultural experience. The essence of a journey by guagua lies in the verbal exchanges with its driver, absorbing the cameraderie of your fellow-travellers, and appreciating the cultural experience of sitting next to a man holding onto a cockerel while you listen (or try not to listen) to the *merengue* music blasting out of decrepit speakers. With its inevitable joking and laughter, the guagua is the ultimate vehicle for making contact with the Dominican people, and at the end of the journey you will find yourself admiring their zest for living even in the face of lifelong poverty.

A less-welcome result of this exuberance is the large amount of accidents involving guaguas. The drivers drink, they go too fast in order to earn more money, they seldom maintain their vehicles properly, and they race each other to relieve the boredom of the journey.

Camionetas.

In rural areas off the network of tarmac roads, locally-operated camionetas provide the public transport. These are normally open-top pick-up trucks, nowadays built in Japan. If you're a woman you can expect to be offered a seat in the cab, but male tourists occasionally have this privelege merely because they're foreigners. The men normally travel in the back, with sacks of rice, bunches of bananas, the local people, and any animals also in transit — and there's plenty of room for your luggage. Look for a convenient bag of rice for your seat.

During the rains the passengers pull a canvas cover, *una lona,* over themselves and the cargo, with each person holding onto his share of it. But in the sunshine a camioneta ride is an excellent way of seeing the countryside, and getting some snatch off-beat photos.

A fun-run by camioneta is the road from Higuey to Macao beach, which takes about an hour and costs RD$3.

Motoconchos.

Motoconchos, or motor-cycle taxis, usually 50cc Hondas, operate in towns where they provide an extremely cheap and convenient method of transport. The motoconcho is particularly useful when you're in town at night and want to go from this disco to that bar; jump onto the nearest motoconcho and tell its driver to go *con brisas* — with the breeze — then hold on for another sampling of life as it is led in the Dominican Republic. The driver will oblige by going the wrong way along one-way streets and by ignoring the traffic lights, and at journey's end will ask for a fare that never exceeds a peso.

The motoconcho is now a part of the daily life of the country, having replaced the donkey in the towns. And, as with the donkey, it has become the centre of much Dominican humour. Don't worry about not finding space for your luggage on a motoconcho — I have seen them carrying refrigerators or even a complete family!

Motor rickshaw. A tourist variation of the motoconcho exists in Samaná, where the vehicle has been expanded to include an enclosed two-wheel trailer with seating for three passengers, making it similar to the motorised rickshaw of the Orient.

Taxis and *Carros Públicos*

The only places you are likely to find conventional taxis are in Santo Domingo city and Las Américas Airport. In the city, there are hotel taxis which have fixed fares and ply for trade from stands near the big hotels. The fares are high, the price you pay for instant availability.

The capital also has private door-to-door taxis which offer a round-the-clock service and are cheaper than hotel taxis, particularly for travelling to the airport. Here are six operators:

Taxi La Paloma, ✆562.3460   Taxi Fácil, ✆685.2202
Taxi Radio, ✆562.1313   Central de Taxi, ✆560.9071−2
Taxi Aguila, ✆686.2547   Taxi Carro, ✆565.0832.

Carros Públicos. Among Santo Domingo's many problems is the absence of a proper system of public transport. No metro, no regular bus schedules — nothing. You are therefore forced to use the carros públicos — the name means 'public cars' in South American Spanish — which are beaten-up saloon cars that charge along the main thoroughfares of the city. They follow set routes, which makes life difficult for the tourist who will not have sufficient knowledge of the city to understand where the carro público is going.

The only solution is to have a general idea of your destination and wave down a carro. If it stops, shout out where you want to go, and maybe you'll be in luck. If not, try again. Once aboard you'll be surprised at the ridiculously small fare, never more than 50 centavos.

There is a half-way stage between a carro público and a taxi — the 'carrera.' If you have the fortune to be the first passenger in a carro público and want to keep it to yourself, tell the driver you want a carrera, a 'private ride.' Instantly you have your own taxi to take you wherever you want — but the fare goes up proportionately.

Buses in Santo Domingo. There *are* buses that run on set routes in Santo Domingo, but if you can work out the routes and use the buses, you have more stamina than I!

CAR and MOTOR-CYCLE RENTAL:
Car rental

The North American influence shows itself strongly in the car rental business — until you look at the rates. Among the better known rental agencies are National, Budget, Hertz, and Rent-a-Wreck, the latter probably having nothing but its name in common with similar firms in the USA; the locally-known agencies include Nelly and Honda.

There are many rental companies across the Dominican Republic, especially in the tourist areas, and it is a growing industry as shown by the fact that eight companies have offices in Las Américas Airport just beyond the customs hall.

This is a typical tariff for an unlimited mileage (*sin kilometraje*) rental:

	DAILY			**WEEKLY**			**MONTHLY**		
	RD$	US$	£	RD$	US$	£	RD$	US$	£
small car or jeep (Suzuki)	325	52	32	1,950	310	195	7,800	1,240	780
large van (Nissan)	450	70	45	2,700	430	270	10,800	1,641	1,080

The mininum-rental time at the daily rate is two days.

The tariff for renting a vehicle with mileage (*con kilometraje*) rates is between 7% and 10% less than the free mileage rate, but you must pay, in the example of the Suzuki above, 30 centavos (4.7¢, 3p) per *kilometer* (not per mile) for the distance you cover.

Insurance. Check the type of insurance offered and make certain you understand it — the paperwork is in English and Spanish — with particular emphasis on the point that many companies expect the customer to pay for all damage up to the cost of RD$3,000 (US$477, £300); this clause means that the cost of insurance is reduced. Insurance? You'll have third-party (PAI) cover, and CDW (collision damage waiver) for all claims beyond the base figure.

As you are not in the USA, always check that the vehicle is in a fair state — you'll seldom be offered one in showroom condition. Check that the tyres aren't bald — they sometimes are — and that you have a spare. Check the tool kit. Check the tank is full of gasoline. Check the doors lock. Check the headlights. And if it's a jeep you're renting, check that it has a complete canvas fold-up roof, otherwise driving in the rain will be a misery.

Car rental in the Dominican Republic is not as cheap as in the

United States, which creates extra demand for the smaller and cheaper vehicles; if you're in this market you would be wise to reserve a car several days before you need it.

Regulations. Most car-hire firms insist that the driver be at least 25 years old, and you may be asked to prove your age; you will in any event need to show your passport and your domestic driving licence — an International Licence is not needed. You will need a credit card of an acceptable name to pay the deposit: you don't leave the card, but you do leave the credit agreement signed, with only the final sum to be added when you return the car, as you would do in the USA.

This list of rental agencies centres on the cities where the tourist is most likely to need them:

Santo Domingo:
Auto Rental, Ortega Gasset 34, ✆565.7873
Avis, Av Abraham Lincoln, ✆533.3530
Budget, Av John F. Kennedy, ✆567.0173
Hertz, Av Independencia, ✆688.2277
Honda, Av John F. Kennedy, ✆567.1015
McDeal, Av George Washington 105, ✆688.6518
National, Av Abraham Lincoln 1056, ✆562.1444
Nelly, José Contreras 139, ✆532.7346
Rentauto, Av 27 de Febrero 247, ✆566.7221

Puerto Plata:
Abby, John F. Kennedy 23, ✆586.2516 — 3995
Budget, Av L. Ginebra, ✆586.4433 —4480; airport ✆586.0284
Nelly, Carr Luperón km3½, ✆586.4888; airport ✆586.0505
McDeal, airport, ✆586.0334
National, Hotel Dorado Naco, ✆586.2019; airport ✆586.0285
Trixy, Av Circunvalación Sur, ✆586.4251

La Romana:
Honda, Av Santa Rosa 83, ✆556.3834
Nelly, Av Santa Rosa 61, ✆556.2156
Monetaria, Esq. Pedro Abreu, Santa Rosa, ✆556.3232
Rentauto, C/ Castillo Marquez 35, ✆556.4181

Advance booking. The international companies will accept bookings made in their branch offices in Europe and North America; ask your travel agency to do it as it gets a commission on the sale. From the USA you can make a reservation yourself direct in the Dominican Republic by calling the relevant toll-free number; Budget, for example, is on ✆800.527.0700.

Motor-cycle rental

Motor-cycle rental companies are opening up all over the country in response to the growing demand for something cheaper than cars;

motor-bikes also offer a convenient means of transport in this warm climate, and over roads which are in a poor state of repair.

The most popular machines are 125cc Suzuki, Yamaha or Honda trials bikes, but 50cc Hondas are better suited for getting around town. The larger hotels hire small motor-bikes — *pasolitas* — to their guests for going down to the beach or to the local restaurant.

Regulations. When you're in charge of a motor-bike you must carry your driving licence, the machine's documents — and you must wear a crash-helmet to conform with the law. You *did* bring one with you from home?

Hazards. The motor-cyclist's major worry is theft of his machine. Never leave it in the street at night under any circumstances, and during the day secure it with the chain and padlock provided. It's not provided? Then you'd better buy a padlock and chain, *un candado y una cadena,* in a general store. The majority of tourist hotels have a patio where you can leave the machine at night — securely locked.

In remote areas punctures can be a problem, as the nearest puncture repair man, *gomero,* will probably be some distance away. Try to carry a spare inner tube, *una cámara de aire,* even if you have to buy it; equip yourself with the appropriate tools if they're not provided — you can bring some of these from home — and don't forget the hand-operated *bomba.* That's a pump, by the way.

The cost. The cost is so much less than car hire that it's convenient to pay by cash, and ready money might give you the opportunity to negotiate a small discount from the weekly rate. There is no mileage rate — but check your insurance.

Watch out! This is American-style baseball!

Santo Domingo:		
	DAILY	**WEEKLY**
Suzuki 125cc trial Suzuki 125cc road	RD$50, US$8, £5 RD$55, US$9, £5.50	RD$315, US$50, £30 RD$350, US$56, £5

Companies: FH★, Bolívar 68, ✆688.1612
      E & E Rent-a-Motor, José Contreras 49, ✆532.6252

Puerto Plata:		
Yamaha DT 125cc trial	RD$175, US$27.80, £17.50	RD$1,050, US$167, £105

Companies: Andrés, Beller 125, ✆586.1623 − 3889
      Helmet, lock and chain included
      Yuyo Rent-a-Motor, Av 12 de Julio 123

Samaná:		
	12 HRS	**24 HRS**
Suzuki 125cc trial	RD$75, US$12, £7.50	RD$100, US$16, £10

Company: Samaná Rent-a-Motor, Malecón, ✆538.2556

Sosúa:		
80cc 125cc		RD$60, US$9.10, £6 RD$110, US$17.60, £11

Sample company: George's Rent-a-Motor, Casa Criolla, C/ Pedro Clisante, ✆571.3050
      There are many rental companies; shop around.

Boca Chica: A rent-a-bike company operates near western roundabout; 125cc trials bikes at RD$150, US$24, £15 for 24 hrs.

★ FH is pronounced 'effeh-acheh.'

Gasoline. Gasoline − petrol − is very cheap in the Dominican Republic, and is sold by the US gallon which is 17% smaller than the imperial gallon. The current price is RD$3.60 (US$0.57¢, £0.36p), which converts to £0.43 per imperial gallon, or US$0.15 (£0.09) per litre.

Petrol stations are open until late in the evening on the approach roads to every important town and, in rural areas where there is no gas station, fuel is sold from roadside stalls. Most stations have their own generator to operate the pumps when the public electricity supply is not working, but some pump the gasoline by hand. Frustratingly, a few simply shut up shop.

Gas stations occasionally run out of supplies, so it's not wise to get down to the red sector on your fuel gauge though you needn't go to the other extreme and carry spare cans of petrol.

Motoring hazards. As cars are so incredibly expensive, most Dominicans keep their vehicles far beyond normal life expectancy, which means there are many dangerous vehicles on the roads. The police have a relaxed approach to the problem, probably because enforcement of stricter regulations would send too many vehicles to the scrap yards. The lesson is plain: *drive carefully*. Be prepared to find, for example, cars driven at night without any lights at all.

The standard of driving is also particularly bad in the Dominican Republic, giving further cause for the visiting motorist to be careful. The driver you are following may suddenly swerve across the road without checking in his mirror – if he has one: he's avoiding an unexpected hole in the road. And the driver following you may suddenly overtake on the wrong side. Traffic lights and rules of priority at junctions are sometimes ignored, and few people bother to use their indicators. As a large minority of motorists never bother with insurance, do your best not to become involved in an accident.

Horses and cattle left grazing untethered by the roadside will wander into the carriageway without warning – and they seem to do it more often on blind corners.

In the urban area the driver who gets where he wants to go is the driver who is most aggressive. Be courteous, and you'll wait for ever for somebody to give way and let you into the traffic. But be a Dominican, and you'll force your way out of the side-road, using your car as a battering-ram or a shield – which further adds to the generally deplorable state of the vehicles.

Driving in Santo Domingo. You like watching horror movies? Why not take part in one for a change – drive a car in the capital city! But if you're the timid type, or merely want to arrive unscathed, then I suggest you avoid Santo Domingo altogether unless you know your route very well, taking the hazards of the one-way system into account. The ultimate horror is when a power cut hits the city and all the traffic lights go blank.

Motoring regulations. Your driving licence is valid for 90 days, after which time foreigners are supposed to apply for a Dominican licence, though this rule exists more in theory than in practice. You are, however, required by law to carry all your motoring documents at all times.

The wearing of **seat belts** is not compulsory; most cars don't have any. But it is a legal requirement to wear a crash-helmet on a motorcycle, although few people bother. You should bring your own helmet if you plan to rent a machine.

Police are vigilant about enforcing the **speed limits,** which are 40kph (25mph) in urban areas and 80kph (50mph) on the open road — but beware the sudden 60kph (37mph) limit. Speed limits are badly indicated, and the police make good use of the fact. The rule of the road is, of course, to **drive on the right.**

Toll roads. Some roads out of Santo Domingo have tolls, the price for a car being 50 centavos. Try to have some small change handy.

Other forms of transport

Bicycles. Scarcely anybody in the Dominican Republic uses a pedal cycle, and my feeling is that it is a particularly dangerous form of transport. Car and guagua drivers hoot motor-cyclists and donkeys off the road, often forcing them into the gutter, so I fear for the future of the ordinary cyclist.

Horses. The horse is the supreme mode of transport in the countryside and Dominicans are superb riders; the large number of horses still used for riding sets this Caribbean island apart from the others.

Young children are brought up in the saddle or, more often, on the bare back of a horse. Don't be surprised to see an eight-year-old child in full control of a huge steed galloping along the side of the road, yet without saddle, stirrups or reins. Leather saddles are expensive in this poor country and those you see are usually in Wild West cowboy style

At sundown this street in La Romana will burst into life.

with a high pommel; much more common is the home-made saddle ingeniously fashioned from straw and cloth.

Horse-riding is becoming a major tourist activity as an increasing number of hotels offer riding lessons and invest in 'ranches' where visitors can go for an hour-long session with an escorted party; this is certainly a good introduction to life in the saddle. For the more adventurous and experienced rider, the Dominican Republic is an equestrian paradise; you can negotiate with any villager for the hire of a horse by the day, the week, or the month. The animals vary in condition, but the price is invariably cheap.

Organised excursions

There are many tour operators in the Dominican Republic offering a variety of organised excursions to various points of interest; this is the solution for the visitor who wants a holiday without making it an adventure.

The main starting-places for these excursions are Santo Domingo and Puerto Plata, but the smaller resorts, and all the big tourist hotels, are in contact with the operators.

While the package visitor will have the full range offered to him or her, the independent traveller must make his own arrangements, either by booking through a tourist hotel or by contacting the tour operator direct. If money is no problem, you can even arrange to have a tour tailored to your own needs and be its only customer.

Sample tours. The standard excursions include:

A tour of the city of Santo Domingo, with historic sights and shopping centres.

The capital by night, taking in a floorshow such as that at the Hotel Jaragua, or some of the casinos.

La Romana, with a visit to Altos de Chavón or a boat journey to Catalina Island and its magnificent beach.

Puerto Plata, including historic sights, shopping, and possibly by cable car to the top of Isabel de las Torres.

Prices are reasonable, with the minimum for the city tour of the capital being US$15, £9.20.

Tour operators:

Bibi Tours, José Contreras 98, Sto Domingo, ✆532.7141

Dimargo Tours, Lope de Vega 16, Sto Domingo, ✆562.7461

Dorado Travel, Juan Sánchez Ramirez – Máximo Gómez (Hotel Caribe I), Sto Domingo, ✆688.6664, 689.9724

Magna Tours, Av Rómul Betancourt 407, Sto Domingo, ✆532.8267, 533.4897

Maritisant Agencia de Viajes, (Travel agent, offers trips to national parks at reasonable prices), Duarte 2, Sto Domingo, ✆685.7910

Metro Tours, Av Winston Churchill, Sto Domingo, ✆567.3138

Omni Tours, Roberto Pastoriza 204, Sto Domingo, ✆566.4228
President Tours, Rómulo Betancourt 1258, 1218, Sto Domingo, ✆533.4455; Plaza Quisqueya, Juan Dolio, ✆529.8686
Prieto Tours, Av Francia 125, Sto Domingo, ✆688.5715; Puerto Plata, ✆586.3988
Puerto Plata Tours, (specialist in tours in the locality), Beller 70, Puerto Plata, ✆586.3858
Santo Domingo Tours, Lope de Vega 17, Sto Domingo, ✆ 562.4865 — 4870
Servicio Turístico Dominicano, (offers tours along the north coast, Cibao and mountains), Plaza Turisol, Puerto Plata, ✆586.5204 —5283; Sto Domingo, ✆535.7501; Sosúa, ✆571.3151 — 2665
Thomas Tours, (caters for large groups such as conventions), Pedro Enrique Ureña 170, Sto Domingo, ✆687.8645; 688.2562
Tropical Tours, Santa Rosa 1, La Romana, ✆556.2512 —2636; Casa de Campo, La Romana, ✆556.3636
Turinter, (operates in many large hotels offering variety of tours), Leopoldo Navarro 4, Sto Domingo, ✆685.4020
Viajes Bohio, Benito Monción 161, Sto Domingo, ✆682.7066; 687.1912
Viajes Continente, J.I. Mañon 29, Sto Domingo, ✆532.0825
Vimenca Tours, Av Abraham Lincoln 306, Sto Domingo, ✆533.9362; Puerto Plata, ✆586.3883

Internal charter flights

All internal flights in the Dominican Republic are charter; there are no scheduled services.

Private flights leave from Santo Domingo's Herrera★ Airport, ✆567.1195 −3900, near Avenida Luperón on the west of the city. Other usable airports are the main Las Américas★ field, and airstrips at Barahona, Cabo Rojo★ at Pedernales, Constanza, Dajabón, Higuey, Casa de Campo★ at La Romana, Monte Cristi, Puerto Plata★, Punta Cana, Samaná and Santiago.

★At these airfields radiocommunication is in English as well as Spanish, so you may charter and pilot your own plane provided you have your pilot's licence. But don't expect impressive organisation as in the less important airstrips foreigners are rare visitors.

Charter companies. Companies that operate charter services:
Fasa Taxi Aereo, ✆567.1195
Servicios Aereos Turisticos, ✆562.2351 −7181
Transporte Aereo, ✆566.2141
Unicharter, ✆567.0481

With Unicharter a single-engine three-seat plane costs RD$1,140 (US$180, £115) to charter from Santo Domingo to Puerto Plata; a twin-engine seven-seater on the same route costs RD$2,700 (US$430, £270). Both fares are one-way.

8: ACCOMMODATION

Tourist or Dominican?

THE DOMINICAN REPUBLIC has a wide range of accommodation for the tourist, from top-class hotels to rustic *cabañas* (cabins) with wooden walls and thatched roofs — but beware the motels: they can be brothels in disguise.

The availability obviously depends on where you are; there is no hotel of quality in Constanza in the mountains — though maybe there is a market for one — and at Macao Beach your only option is Don Coco's Cabañas. On the other hand, if you're looking for budget accommodation by the beach in Puerto Plata or Bavaro, you will be disappointed: you merely have the choice of several comparatively expensive and luxurious tourist hotels.

Tourist hotels

Tourist hotels in the Dominican Republic are no different from those in any other international resort, with all services as perfect as the mass-throughput will allow. Some visitors spend their entire holiday within the grounds of these mini-resorts, totally unaware of the country and the people that lie just beyond the gates.

The reason is obvious. Here the package traveller has a room with hot water permanently on tap, and lights that never fail, thanks to the hotel's standby generator. He or she has a private bedroom, a restaurant with menus that offer safe, international cuisine, and staff who speak English — as well as French, Italian and occasionally German. Indeed, the staff are the only Dominicans who set foot inside these hotels as the rates are prohibitively high for the locals, starting at around US$20 per person per night and peaking above US$100.

Taxes. The independent traveller can try his luck at such a hotel for a night or two, risking the possibility of mass bookings, but if this is for you, check that the price quoted includes all taxes: the 10% service tax, the 6% sales tax, and the 5% hotel rooms tax.

There were 16,000 tourist hotel rooms in the republic in 1989, increasing to 22,500 by the end of 1990.

Tourist hotels are almost exclusively on beachfront sites, and their presence virtually removes all other types of lodging from the locality.

Dominican hotels

Middle-class Dominicans on business or on holiday stay in the less ostentatious hotels which were there long before the tourist explosion; these are similar to the premises you will find if you wander two, three or four streets inland from the beach in any Spanish Mediterranean resort.

The problem is that they are not found in every town, so what could have been an agreeable standard for the visitor touring the country, becomes instead an occasional oasis of comfort.

Many of these hotels are charming, full of character, and exude a sense of history; particularly the Hotel Mercedes in Santiago. But you must shop carefully, avoiding those with a night-club or discotheque on the premises, and making certain you don't choose a brothel masquerading as a hotel.

Typically, the staff in these hotels is good-natured and speaks nothing but Dominican Spanish. You should expect to pay between RD$40 and RD$100 (US$6.40–US$16, £4–£10) for a double room, but your bathroom may be private or shared, you may have a big ceiling fan or air-conditioning or neither of them, and the restaurant may be working – or it may not. But that is all part of the appeal of this fascinating country.

In the capital, some old buildings have been renovated into hotels for middle-class Dominicans; keep an eye open for the Hostal Nader.

Trujillo's hotels. In the 1950s, Rafael Trujillo, the republic's dictator and self-promoted general, ordered the building of a chain of nine hotels in an attempt to promote tourism. The plan failed, but the hotels still haunt the countryside like a scattered herd of white elephants, often in places where adventurous tourists would want to visit.

Trujillo's structures are now known as state hotels and are due to be renovated by Corphotels, a local enterprise. They could become interesting places for stopovers in the near future but at the moment they merely emphasise Trujillo's obsession with blocks of concrete or look like sets for horror films because of their decadent grandeur and emptiness. But they're cheap, and they always have rooms to rent.

Apart-hotels

The apart-hotel is a useful invention and may be of interest to the tourist looking for something out of the ordinary. It combines features of a rented apartment with the services of a hotel; for example, you have a fully-furnished bedroom and living room, a fully-equipped kitchen, and a patio for hanging out your washing. It goes beyond the Europeans' self-catering chalet or the Americans' efficiency motel as it also offers maid service, and normally a guard to keep an eye on your transport.

An apart-hotel is an excellent alternative to the tourist hotel for fairly long stays. While you may be able to take a room for one night – expect to pay from US$10 to US$15 – it's always preferable to make reservations for any lengthy stay, remembering that in many apart-hotels the residents are students or wokers on medium to long-term tenancies, while other hotels specialise in suites large enough for long-term family oppupation. The longer you stay, of course, the greater your discount.

Guest houses and *pensiones*

At the bottom end of the market the guest houses and *pensiones* offer an intimate glimpse of life as lived by the average Dominican: in Santo Domingo's crowded districts it may occasionally be too intimate.

You will be able to find a cheap bed for the night in a nondescript guest house anywhere in the country; all you need do is let people know you are looking and you will soon be pointed in the right direction.

The accommodation will be spartan, the bathroom shared either with other guests or with the resident family – and you can interpret 'bathroom' in the American as well as the British sense. The hygiene will depend on whether there's a resident old matron in the house: if there isn't, the place might be dirty. The sign *Pensión familiar* ('family' guest house) suggests the presence of the old matron and infers a higher standard of cleanliness.

Light and water. The *pensión familiar* sign cannot guarantee hot water on tap, and frequently you will rely on a bucket of water in the shower room. In the absence of a private generator the electricity supply may fail at any time, so you must keep a torch handy throughout the night.

The character of a pensión depends largely on which town it's in. In

The loading jetty at Sabana de la Mar; it's no surprise cars can't take this ferry to Samaná.

small communities it may be a charming place full of character and friendliness; your vehicle will be looked after, and you may wake in the morning to a free cup of coffee. In Santo Domingo you may be sharing a room with several people, mostly Dominicans, forcing you to try your Spanish, but in return you may be invited out to a drink or to a dance – though it could all be at your expense.

The cost? From RD$15 to RD$25 per person per night (US$2.40 – $4, £1.50 – £2.50).

Hotel-restaurants and motels

Beware! Often the motel or hotel-restaurant you see on the outskirts of a large town is used solely as a brothel for some extra-marital sex or for the services of a prostitute.

In consequence, the rooms may be incredibly sleazy with red satin sheets, heart-shaped pillows with lace frills, and mirrored walls, and the rental is quoted not only for the night but by the hour; I understand the short rentals are based on a set six-hour rate after which you're expected to be out. Customers wanting less than the set period ask for *un rato,* 'a while,' but for the six-hour session beginning around midnight, customers rent *para amanecer,* 'to go through to daybreak.'

The motel-in-disguise can even be found in the smaller town, where it occasionally masquerades as a *cabaña,* and is sometimes equipped with connecting drive-in garages with remote-control doors. I don't think you'll be interested in the tariff.

Cabañas

A cabaña is a wooden hut that is traditionally thatched with leaves. Tourist versions of the cabaña are quite comfortable and provide an alternative to the conventional hotel room, particularly on beachside sites at Macao in the east and Baoruco in the south. Now forget mains water and electricity and imagine the cabaña to be your permanent home, and you have a good indication of the living conditions of most of the Dominican people. Sadly, a number of tourist hotels now offer concrete bungalows under the description of 'cabaña,' which is blatant misrepresentation.

Camping

The Dominican Republic is normally too hot for most tents to be comfortable unless they're large – and those are difficult things to carry without transport. There are no campsites in the country so camping would need to be in the open countryside. My feeling is that the one place where a tent would be an advantage is on the beautiful, wild east coast beaches in winter, when it's pleasantly cool. In fact, camping is the only option along this coastline.

9: DINING OUT AND NIGHTLIFE

Rum and merengue

THE DOMINICAN REPUBLIC is a magnificent hothouse for fruit and vegetables, with a wide selection of both, nurtured by the perfect climate. Fresh fruit is always available, with one variety following another as the seasons change.

The people eat plenty of meat, mostly beef, pork and goat; sea food is less common and tends to be sea bass, or shrimps or lobster for the wealthy.

Dominicans are very good cooks, adept at preparing the country's standard dishes: rice and beans; a stew known as *sancocho;* roast pork; pieces of fried chicken; and fried bananas. These dishes are delicious and form the basis of *la cocina criolla,*, 'Creole cuisine,' yet after considering the wide range of vegetables, fruits and sea food available I have decided that Dominicans are quite happy to eat three or four dishes all their lives and not experiment. You will seldom come across the use of hot spices or unexpected combinations in Dominican cuisine as you would in Mexican cooking, though the tourist boom is already exerting its influence in the tourists' own restaurants.

Comida criolla. The predominant food is *comida criolla,* 'Dominican food,' even in non-tourist restaurants which proclaim themselves as Chinese or Italian. Don't expect 'Chinese' to mean the same in the Dominican Republic as it does in the USA or Europe: to the simple peasant anything that isn't *comida criolla* is suspicious.

Despite this lack of variety, which is even more evident in the smaller towns, I feel that if you shop around you may find some of the best food you will ever eat, judged by quality and price.

Fruits. Fruit is plentiful in the markets, and is exceptionally cheap. In season, look out for pineapple (*piña*), melon and water-melon, mango, banana (both the familiar yellow type, known in the Dominican Republic as *guineo,* and the hard green *plátano* used for frying), papaya (*lechosa,*) a type of grapefruit known as *toronja,* orange (*china*), coconut (*coco*), passion fruit (*chinola*), and soursop (*guanabana*), a fruit which looks like the spiked ball at the end of a medieval mace-and-chain; it's white flesh is used to make milkshakes.

These are just a few appetizers from the extensive list of Dominican fruits; among the many others that are unknown in the English-speaking world are *zapote*, *tamarindo* and *nispero*. Fruits are delicious in milkshakes, (*batidas*), or in fruit salads, (*ensaladas de frutas,*) with lime juice, (*jugo de limón,*) sprinkled over them.

Salads and vegetables. Dominicans don't make complicated salads. They use lettuce or shredded cabbage, tomato — usually green — onion, and avocado, (*aguacate*). For vegetable salads they use plenty of tubers such as yam (*yuca*) and sweet potato (*papa dulce*) which are filling in their own right and, when prepared with butter, are fattening as well.

Rice is the staple diet in the Caribbean, and the Dominican Republic is no exception. In *arroz con habichuelas* the rice is fortified by pouring on red beans in their cooking juice; the next day the left-overs are fried until dry, when they become *moro*.

Plantain fried in slices to become *tostones*, the Dominican equivalent of Britain's chips and the USA's French fries, accompany almost every meal, and breakfast is often egg mashed with plantain. The name, *mangú*, sounds very descriptive: goo.

Meats. Chicken is very popular and is usually fried in tasty little morsels known as *chicharrones*. Pork is often served the same way, similar to the scratchings that originated in northern England, although the accepted way to eat pork is at a party where you slice parts of meat and fat off a whole roast animal, similar to the *doner kebab* of Turkey. Goat meat is another favourite, often made into the stew *chivo guisado*. You like tripe or fried liver? Then ask for *mondongo* or *bofe*.

Sea foods. Lobster, *langosta*, is prepared either in a garlic sauce after being boiled, or cooked over charcoal *a la plancha*. It is the most expensive sea food in the Dominican Republic but is standard fare in any tourist restaurant.

Conch, *lambí*, which to me is a rubbery-textured mollusc, is delicious when cooked and shredded. Typical preparation is either with vinegar, *a la vinagreta*, or boiled and served with a tasty sauce as *lambí guisado*.

Shrimps proliferate in the north-east where they are delicious and cheap, and are usually served with mayonnaise.

The most common fish is the tasty sea bass, *mero*, with kingfish, *carite*, another favourite. Ask for your fish in *salsa criolla*, a local sauce made from coconut and tomato with other flavourings. A final caution: I've eaten plenty of fish in this country, but visitors who are susceptible to stomach upsets after fish meals should be careful.

Desserts. Dominicans don't have a liking for sweet foods so desserts

Guaguas line up to collect passengers. Try to be first aboard to have a window seat.

are not common; you will probably be offered *dulces*, sweet fruits liquidised and then solidified in a syrup and served in little cubes, or *bizcocho*, a type of pudding or cake made from rice, or simply plain fruit.

The restaurants

There are two main types of restaurant: those catering for the tourist trade and offering a more international menu; and those catering for local custom and serving a comida criolla menu. A fringe third type exists in the Chinese restaurants and pizzerias which attract tourists but which also serve the native population with dishes modified to the local taste.

You have no problem if you want to sample traditional Dominican fare. The cheapest place is a *comedor* — sparse, open to the street, and with a limited choice of food which is displayed in glass cases. Comedors vary; while some offer bargains, others may be passports to upset stomachs. Their target customers are the working population looking for a cheap lunch.

In the remoter towns the comedor is usually the only kind of restaurant, while in the villages the choice is brought down to the roadside *fritura*, an old woman with a cauldron of boiling oil, a table, and a chair or two for the customers; she serves the usual plantains, rice and beans for a few pesos.

The pizzeria is the only foreign introduction that has gained a sizeable share of the Dominican restaurant market. It's a little more sophisticated than the comedor and the customer sits outside under a parasol. Oh, yes — the pizzas are good!

Chimichurri. An alternative to the restaurant is the *chimichurri*, the Dominican version of the hamburger store, where you can buy a pork sandwich — *sandwich de pierna* — or a chimichurri itself; they're tasty and very cheap.

International cuisine. The more international your gastronomic demands become, the more you must expect to pay; Chinese restaurants are common and offer good value, but the Chinese influence is almost non-existent. Arabic food is a little more expensive, but fairly common in the cities, while French cuisine is considered to be the most sophisticated and therefore the most expensive. By contrast, South American food is rare.

Hygiene. The level of hygiene in restaurants is reasonable, but don't expect to get US or European standards without paying the appropriate price. People liable to stomach upsets should avoid the frituras as their cooking oil is used many times, and visitors should always be careful about eating fish in any but the tourist hotels' own restaurants unless they are absolutelty certain that it is fresh; the frequent failures in the public electricity supply mean that frozen fish may have been unfrozen once or twice.

Vegetarians. The Dominican Republic's restaurants are not normally equipped to serve vegetarian dishes, but in the capital city there are several able to cope, such as 'Ananda' at C/ Casimiro de Moya 7, Gazcue, 'La Terraza El Terrenal' on the Malecón, 'Bethel' at C/ Gral Luperón 9, and 'Govinda' at C/ Gaetano Rodriguez, also in Gazcue. Most of these places are motivated by ideological groups such as Hare Krishna.

Tipping. Tipping in local restaurants is discretionary. You give if you want to, and you give what you feel the service deserved.

Service. In most places the waiters are quick to attend, but if you feel it's time you had some service it's quite normal behaviour to clap your hands to attract the waiter's attention.

So what's available in a Dominican restaurant? This sample menu is from Willy's Restaurant, Puerto Plata, with prices valid for 1989.

Bebidas — **Beverages**

Cuba libre, rum with Coca-Cola	RD$5, 80¢, 50p
Piña colada	RD$8, US$1.30, 80p
Vodka tonic	RD$8, US$1.30, 80p
Cerveza, beer, *pequeña*, small	RD$5, 80¢, 50p
— *grande*, large	RD$8, US$1.30, 80p
Jugos naturales, fruit juices	RD$3, 48¢, 30p
Refrescos, soft drinks	RD$2.50, 40¢, 25p

Desayuno — **Breakfast**
Huevos fritos, fried eggs .... RD$6, 95¢, 60p
Tortilla de jamón y queso, ham & cheese omelet ....
RD$12, US$1.30, £1.20

Ensalada — **Salad**
Ensalada verde, green salad .... RD$4, 64¢, 40p

Sandwichs — **Sandwiches**
Sandwich de jamón y queso, ham & cheese sandwich . RD$6, 95¢, 60p
Sandwich de pollo, chicken sandwich .... RD$7, US$1.10, 70p
Hamburger .... RD$7, US$1.10, 70p

Entradas — **Entrées**
Croqueta de pollo, chicken croquette .... RD$10, US$1.60, £1
Popurri de mariscos, seafood pot-pourri .... RD$17, US$2.70, £1.70
Sopa de cebolla, onion soup .... RD$4, 64¢, 40p

Platos fuertes — **Main courses**
Espaguettis a la Bolognesa, spaghetti Bolognese ....
RD$17, US$2.70, £1.70
Langosta a la parrilla, roasted lobster .... RD$75, US$12, £7.50
Camarones al ajillo, shrimps in garlic sauce ..... RD$60, US$9.55, £3.60
Arroz con pollo, rice with chicken .... RD$15, US$2.40, £1.50
Mero a la criolla, Creole seabass .... RD$30, US$4.80, £3.30
Filet miñon, ... RD$35, US$5.60, £3.50
Chicharrones de pollo, fried chicken .... RD$18, US$2.90, £1.80
Lambí, conch meat .... RD$22, US$3.50, £2.20

Postres — **Desserts**
Dulce de naranja, orange sweet-cake .... RD$4, 64¢, 40p
Helado, ice cream .... RD$5, 80¢, 50p
Café .... RD$2, 32¢, 20p

Drinks

Among the selection of **non-alcoholic drinks,** all the fruit juices and
milkshakes are of excellent value. In Santo Domingo and most areas of
the Cibao — the Yaque del Norte valley up to La Vega — fruit juice
sellers are easy to find, but they are less common in the east where
the land produces sugar cane in preference to fruit.

Coconut milk is a refreshing drink that's available everywhere; the
locals claim it is 'good for your kidneys.' Any young lad will climb a
tree to bring down a couple of young, green nuts, the kind that bear
milk, but watch out for the sign *hay coco frío,* where you can buy
them for a peso or two. How to drink it? Ask somebody to slice off the
top with a machete, then drink the milk as from a jug.

Frío frío. In most towns, and especially in Santo Domingo, you'll

A 'frío frío' comes to the rescue of a thirsty local.

come upon the *Frío frío* ('cold, cold'), a man pushing a cart full of bottles of coloured liquids, and a huge block of ice at which he continually chips. For a peso he'll put a quantity of crushed ice in a plastic cup and pour on the fruit flavour of your choice. It's delicious, and in the heat and fumes of the capital it's doubly welcome. But those visitors with weak stomachs should remember the vital point: he will have used tap water to make his ice.

Alcohol. The Dominican Republic is, above all else, a rum drinkers' paradise. Rum is tippled at all times of the day, and in all sorts of ways, quite often neat and straight from the bottle. The locals spend hours in debating which rum is best – Barceló, Bermudez or Siboney, or any of the fifty other brands which come from the country's six distilleries. They are all cheap, and any one of them can give you a good hangover until you're accustomed to it.

I find the **piña colada** is a wonderful drink, a mixture of pineapple juice, coconut juice, rum, and ice; the same thing without the pineapple is a *coco loco* – 'crazy coconut.' Other wonders are rum punch – pronounced *ron ponch* – Cuba libre (rum with Coca-Cola or Seven Up) and rum *a la roca*, 'on the rocks.'

Beer. The Dominican Republic produces three very good and very cheap beers – Quisqueya, Presidente and Bohemia – and you can also buy Heineken, which is more expensive. Beer is sold in ice-cold bottles, either *grande* or *pequeña*, and it is a point of honour to complain if the beer is not cold enough; any consciencious waiter who has served you a slightly warm beer is humbled with shame if you point it out to him. All bottles are served with a paper serviette wrapped around the base — to prevent your hand getting cold? Or to stop the bottle dripping? Your guess is as good as mine.

The bohío restaurant. A *bohío* is a typical Dominican structure used as a simple shelter, nowadays often covering a dance floor or used as a restaurant. Half a dozen poles each with one end buried in the ground, support a simple, circular thatched roof, usually with no walls.

Nightlife

The Dominican Republic is geared towards enjoyment, and going out at night is as necessary as breathing to the average Dominican. Friday, Saturday and Sunday are the main nights for fun, but he can be socially active on midweek evenings as well, especially between six and nine.

A night out normally involves drinking, dancing, and just relaxing from the worries of poverty or unemployment. Dancing is the Dominicans' greatest passion, and as a nation they must be the world's greatest dancers. The Dominican male may live in poverty or be illiterate, but on the dance floor he reigns supreme, and he knows it.

Men always dance with a female partner, and the interplay between man and woman is intricate and exciting to watch, raising the question of why these people seem to know how to interpret rhythm so gracefully.

Merengue. The Dominican Republic's national music is *merengue,* pronounced 'mer-en-gay.' From the moment you set foot in the country until the moment you leave, you'll never be out of its influence. At first you may think all native music sounds the same, but as your ear becomes attuned you'll begin to recognise merengue from other Caribbean rhythms such as *salsa, cumbia, bachata,* and others.

Merengue is almost a religion to the Dominicans and, like a religion, it has its own saints, among whom are Johnny Ventura, Wilfredo and Sigfrido Vargas, and Los Hermanos Rosario.

There are many theories about merengue's origins, but all recognise its beginnings as African rather than Spanish. The guitar doesn't feature in the music as much as one might expect, for that was a symbol of the colonialist bosses. Merengue was, and still is, essentially the music of the Dominican people, who had only the drum, the guira, and the human voice, though over the years the music has begun to accept other cultures, taking in first the French accordion and recently the bass guitar, trumpet and keyboard.

If music is in your heart, you must see a live merengue concert and join in the sheer exuberance of the Dominican spirit at its most liberated. Everyone dances together, everyone drinks together, and the trumpets often play together.

Rules. And why not join in? The social guidelines are simple: a young woman should not dance more than twice with the same man and should not dance *boleros*, slow dances, unless she is serious about her partner; a man should always ask the permission of any Dominican male escort if he wishes to dance with one of the girls. This is an important formality to avoid bruising the macho image.

The other dances. Salsa comes from Puerto Rico and is more difficult than merengue; it's therefore not for you unless you're a natural dancer. Bachata is a beautiful manifestation of woe, of sexual passion or frustration sung to a guitar accompaniment, and it's a favourite among the older men. It's often the music of brothels, and is considered base by those Dominicans who consider themselves to be socially superior.

You can dance in *discotecas* or in dance halls; the latter are drinking saloons, normally open to the air, with a dance floor in the centre surrounded by tables and chairs. Every community in the country has some kind of dance hall.

Nude dancing. Most nightlife is centred on drinking and dancing, in all their combinations and variations; the locations differ, but the action is basically the same. Unless, of course, you want to see a performance of nude women dancers. There are many such places around the country, the most respectable being *Le Petit Château* on Av 30 de Mayo at the western end of the Malecón in Santo Domingo; other nude dancing halls are nothing more than brothels in another disguise.

The cinema

The country has many cinemas, frequently showing English-language films from the USA with Spanish sub-titles; Dominican release is about four months later than American, and for added interest you may occasionally see characters coming back from the dead. No worry — it's merely that the rolls are being projected in the wrong order!

Don't expect silence in the cinema. And do expect to see a number of X-rated porno films on offer.

10: STREETWISE

Race, sex, crime, souvenirs

THE AVERAGE DOMINICAN is *mulato,* a mixture of black and white, with some native Amerind (American Indian as opposed to Asian Indian) blood in remoter parts of the country. The result is a handsome race, and Dominican women were popular entrants in the Miss World contests.

Racial prejudice. Superficially, racism is not apparent, but Dominicans are very colour conscious, normally believing that whiteness is desirable and blackness is a symbol of backwardness and savagery. There are many words to describe skin colour, with *feo* adding 'black' to the 'ugly' that came over from Spain. *Prieto* is 'very black,' *moreno* is 'brown,' *trigeño* light brown, with *blanco* and *gringo* meaning white, in each case change the final −o to −a to apply the adjective to a woman.

Haitians are consequently at the bottom of the colour and racial scale. There are several possible reasons for this, beginning with the historic antagonism with Haiti which has occupied the entire island of Hispaniola twice; and there are the inevitable scars left by slavery which linked whiteness with power, wealth and freedom, and blackness with poverty, ignorance and subservience.

Ignorance also breeds prejudice and, strangely, Dominicans know very little about neighbouring Haiti and have a false idea about what Haitians are like, assuming them all to be stupid, mean, violent and uncivilized. One of the results is the Dominicans' lack of sympathy when they see Haitians working long hours for miserable pay in the cane-fields, and living in extreme poverty. The sad aspect of Dominican racism means that Dominicans are capable of cruelty and injustice to their fellow men.

Gringo. A gringo (gringa) is anybody not from the Dominican Republic and who is white. A gringo is simultaneously respected and despised for his money, is envied for his economic ability to come to this country with nothing to do but spend, and is laughed at in private for his performance on the dance floor and his reluctance to relax and forget about tomorrow. And the Dominican cannot understand the gringo's curiosity for seemingly uninteresting things such as admiring

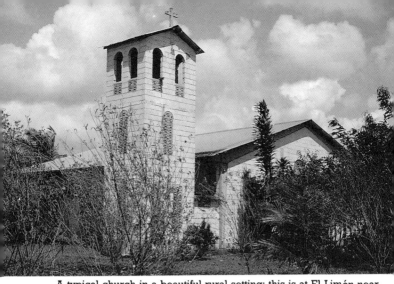

A typical church in a beautiful rural setting; this is at El Limón near Higuey.

plants, buying paintings, and riding in a guagua. Gringo — you're strange!

Dominican-York

Many Dominicans risk their lives in the 75-mile (120km) *Canal de la Mona*, more popularly known as *El Canal de la Muerte*, 'Death Channel,' trying to reach Puerto Rico, the gateway to the promised land of the United States. Most attempt the crossing illegally in ill-equipped, overloaded fishing boats called *yolas* (you can see here the English word 'yawl'); many have sold all they possess to raise the RD$3,000 for the journey, but few get across. Each year hundreds drown or are eaten by sharks when the boat either sinks or drifts off course into the wide Caribbean.

El Dominican-York. Those that cross Death Channel and succeed in reaching the United States as illegal immigrants, usually join the Dominicans community in New York.

And of them, those that make their fortune and manage to gain residence status, may go back to the Dominican Republic to boast of their success — or let their ostentatiously-worn gold chains, bracelets and rings, boast for them. These poor rich people are caught between two cultures and don't identify with either of them, to the point where Dominican-Yorks of my acquaintance talk disparagingly of Dominicans as if they were a race apart.

Crime and violence

There is little gratuitous violence in the country. The tourist can feel safe on the streets of the Dominican Republic; he — and she — is probably safer than in his own country, especially at night. Fights have motives, usually sexual rivalry for a woman, or a squaring of accounts, and attacks against women are more likely to be instances of wife-beating which is unfortunately common.

Danger spots. That doesn't mean there is no risk to the gringo visitor. Be wary of entering carros públicos late at night, particularly in Santo Domingo and especially if there are only a few male passengers: they could be thieves or rapists waiting for an opportunity to strike.

Pickpockets operate in gangs at merengue festivals. The victim is jostled by a group of people supposedly involved in some little affray, and by the time the visitor realises it was all a stunt, his wallet has gone.

Motor-cycles left unattended at night are likely to disappear: always take them off the road and lock them.

Guns. It is illegal to carry a gun on the streets in the Dominican Republic, but many people don't seem to have heard about this law. A gun is a macho symbol, but when carried by a man who has already proved his *machismo* in a bout of rum-drinking, that gun becomes a threat, and it is time for the prudent gringo — and everybody else — to slip quietly out of the bar. I would not stay even when guns are fired into the air in the street as an excess of good spirits: 34 people needed hospital treatment after seeing in the New Year of 1989.

Machetes. In the countryside, men walk with their razor-sharp machetes in their hand. Don't be intimidated by this; it's merely the tool of their trade.

Prostitution. Prostitution is in evidence throughout the Dominican Republic, especially in the tourist areas around Boca Chica, Puerto Plata and La Romana. The girls themselves may proposition their potential clients as well as rely on approaches from their *buscones* (pimps).

Every town has its bars where these girls operate, and the local *cafetería* is a favourite. Dominicans have many other words for a girl who tries to make a living in this way or, as they say, *buscarsela,* favourite options being *avión,* 'aircraft' and *grillo,* 'cricket,' (the insect).

Towns in the Dominican Republic don't have red-light districts; there are little pockets of prostituion scattered everywhere.

Homosexuals. There is a fair tolerance of homosexuality.

Shopping.

Bargaining is the key word when you're buying anything hand-made, and even when you're shopping for clothes in a store. If you want to buy a painting, then bargain — *regatear* — and you may pay 60% less than the initial asking price.In big stores you might take 25% off an item of clothing: it all depends on your skill and how desperate the seller is for money. But don't feel ashamed to bargain: it's the way of life.

Souvenirs. Craft goods are on the increase and there are now some good craft souvenirs to be found in the country. Look for **paintings** in the so-called 'naïve' style, showing subjects such as women in the market place, mountain scenes, cockfights. Local artists will paint whatever is selling, copying the style of the Haitians; indeed, lots of the painters are Haitians living in the Dominican Republic. The quality is not as good as you would find in Haiti, but the price is a lot less. If you plan to buy local art you should consider bringing a cardboard tube to carry it in.

Beautiful **carvings** are made in mahogany (*caoba*), with paler woods used for human and animal abstract forms, and soapstone, a form of talc, is carved into animals or grotesque faces. Prices are extremely reasonable.

One of the Dominican Republic's claims to fame is its **amber,** as the country is second only to the USSR in the wealth of its deposits. Amber — fossilised resin — is a beautiful, honey-coloured semi-precious jewel that is light and warm to the touch, but the price in the Dominican Republic is four or five times cheaper than in Europe even when the finished stone contains a perfectly preserved insect. The amber mines are near Santiago, but you can buy the jewellery anywhere in the country.

Dominican **turquoise,** now known as larimar, is a beautiful stone that has only recently been used in jewellery. Coming from the Barahona region it is a uniquely Dominican souvenir available at a reasonable price.

Black **coral** finds its way into all kinds of jewellery. It's beautiful and cheap, but as its collection damages the coral reefs I recommend you don't buy. The black coral sold on the tourist beaches, by the way, may be plastic.

A final tip. The best place to shop for artisan objects is the Mercado Modelo in C/ Mella near the Parque Independencia in Santo Domingo. Don't forget to bargain!

11: DOMINICAN FACTFILE

Facts at your fingertips

AFFILIATIONS

The Dominican Republic is a member of the Organisation of American States (OAS), and the United Nations Organisation.

ARMED FORCES

The armed forces are divided into the navy, *la Marina*, with 4,000 men; the air force, *las Fuerzas Armadas*, with 3,800; and the army, *el Ejército*, with 20,000. Service is voluntary, for four years.

As in most Latin-American countries the military has played a big role in influencing internal politics, through uprisings, coups and dictatorships. The army became very powerful under Trujillo (16 August 1939 – 30 May 1961) and had a greatly-feared secret police, the SIM, but since those days it has been reduced in size.

The major external military threat is from Haiti which, although poor, has a higher population and historically has always attempted to control the entire island.

BUSINESS HOURS

Banks: Weekdays, 0830-1730; Saturdays, for foreign exchange only, 0800-1200.

Supermarkets: The large supermarkets in Santo Domingo and other major towns are open 0800-2000, Mon-Sat and occasionally Sun, working a straight shift with no lunchtime closure.

Colmados: These neighbourhood convenience stores are open at the times when people are most likely to buy. In rural areas they also serve as bars and are open late into the evening; they are also open on Sunday.

Other shops: Mon-Sat 0900-1200, 1430-1900. Note the 2½-hour siesta.

Post offices: Mon-Fri 0800-1200, 1430-1700; Saturday 0800-1200, 1500-1700.

Codetel (for international telephone calls:) Codetel offices are in every town and are open 0800-2200 or -2400, depending on the town.

DIVORCE

The Dominican Republic specialises in rapid divorces. If you wish to do what Mike Tyson did, or emulate Richard Burton and Elizabeth Taylor, this may be the place for you, too.

You can be divoced in 24 hours provided you have legal papers attesting to mutual consent, and get a Dominican lawyer to present your case. Contact the International Law Offices, Hotel El Embajador, Arcade, Santo Domingo. ✆(809).532.0383; 533.4688; 535.0330; 535.0882. Telex RCA.326.4322. The officers speak English as they do plenty of business with US citizens looking for a 'shotgun divorce.'

DRUGS

Dominican law is very strict on drug control and anybody caught in possesion of drugs can expect harsh treatment. The result is that there are far less narcotics in evidence than in many other countries. I have never been approached by a drug dealer, and you would need to search hard to make contact with the drugs world which exists in the rougher bars in the bigger cities.

Colombian cocaine goes direct to the USA for dollars; I don't think the Dominican peso and the level of poverty have kindled the interest of the drug barons.

EDUCATION

Santo Domingo's first university was established in 1538 making it the oldest in the Americas; it is now the *Universidad Autónoma de Santo Domingo*, the 'Autonomous University.' The country has seven other state-run universities attracting many foreign students.

The Constitution decrees that the State must provide primary education to all children from 7 to 14 years, and offer secondary education to those who want it. Only 68% of children attend primary school and fewer still go on to secondary levels, particularly in the rural areas where there may not be a school, or where the parents don't see the advantage of education. As a result you shouldn't be surprised to see children working as gas station attendants. Adult literacy is estimated to be 23%.

Despite this reduction from the potential demand, many schools operate a rota system as there are not enough classrooms available; you will therefore see children going to and from school at all hours of the day. The plain truth is that the birthrate is too high, as it is in most poor countries.

ELECTRICITY

The country has an electricity-generation problem, which results in many towns having their supply cut off for indefinite periods. This is the main cause of popular discontent with the government, as wealthy people, hotels – particularly those serving the tourist industry – larger shops and many petrol stations, have their own generators.

The system offers 110-120v AC 60-cycles throughout the country, but some industries and hotels also have 220v 60-cycles available.

The plugs and sockets are of US design; Europeans will appreciate knowing the plugs have two pins each 16mm long by 6mm wide and 1.5mm thick, with an 11mm gap between them.

FESTIVALS

There are many, many festivals. These are a few which are of interest to tourists:

New Year's Eve – New Year's Day: on the Malecón in Santo Domingo.

January: 21; Religious pilgrimage to the Basilica of Altagracia in Higuey.

February: 25-27; Carnival in Santo Domingo.

Holy Week, preceding Easter: Spontaneous village and town processions and *gagá* dancing. Gagá is frantic dancing to drums and reed pipes which leads to trance, or may end in a drunken stupor. Many men use this Haitian dance as an excuse to dress as women and abandon all social restrains.

July: 3rd week; Merengue Festival, Santo Domingo, on Malecón.

August: 16; Festival of Santiago.

September: 24; Pilgrimage to the *Sanctuario de la Mercedes*, Santo Cerro, La Vega.

October: 2nd week; Ambar (Amber) Festival of Puerto Plata.

Christmas: Celebrations start on 20th December and run to 30th.

As in Spain, each town has its own patron saint, and a festival in his or her honour. The celebrations last a week and involve lots of drinking and some ethnic and popular dancing. In the countryside, the festivals combine Catholicism with voodoo and African animist rituals.

FLAG

The Dominican Republic's flag (see back cover) has the national coat of arms in the centre; this is a quartered shield flanked by the national banners, scrolls, and an open Bible. An inscription reads *dios, patria, libertad*.

GAS

Camping Gaz or similar brands are not on sale in small cylinders. Rural Dominicans cook on a *fogón*, the traditional camp fire of three small logs and three rocks; this is used even when electricity is available.

GOVERNMENT

The president heads the Dominican Republic's Government, and appoints the Cabinet. The National Legislature, *La Asamblea Legislativa Nacional*, consists of a 27-member Senate and a 120-member Chamber of Deputies, the *Cámara de Diputados*. All civilians who have passed their 18th birthday have the right to vote, electing both a president and a legislature for a four-year term.

The republic is divided into 26 provinces and one *distrito nacional* (the capital and environs), with the president appointing provincial governors and county leaders, but the electorate choosing the leaders of the 100 *municipios*, urban areas.

Turbulent times. The country gained its independence from Spain in 1844 but was under US military occupation from 1916 to 1924, after which the Dominican Republic went through as much political turmoil as the average Latin-American state. In 1930 Rafael Leonidas Trujillo Molina overthrew the elected president, Horacio Vásquez; Trujillo promoted himself to general, and was absolute dictator until 1947 when his brother Héctor took control, holding it until 1960. General Trujillo was assassinated in May 1961, which let his vice-president Dr Joaquín Balaguer into top office.

In December 1961 Balaguer allowed the formation of moderate opposition groups; he resigned two months later and in the presidential election of December 1962, the first in 38 years, Dr Juan Bosch Gaviño was victor. Bosch, exiled since 1930, was founder and leader of the *Partido Revolucionario Dominicano,* and took office in February 1963.

Coup. Seven months later a coup defeated him, and the army put in Emilio de los Santos, but Bosch's supporters led a movement of civil unrest under General Elías Wessin y Wessin, resulting in 23,000 US troops occupying the country until September 1965.

Balaguer was returned in the June 1966 election, and again in May 1970, but in 1973 guerillas landed and he was forced to declare a state of emergency: Bosch went into hiding.

Balaguer was re-elected in May 1974, but lost the 1978 election to the PRD candidate Silvestre Antonio Guzmán Fernández — but *he* committed suicide after allegations of fraud, letting in his vice-president Jacobo Majluta Azar.

But Majluta was considered too old to contest the 1982 elections and the PRD nominee Salvador Jorge Blanco came to office.

Peasants revolt. The next year the peasants occupied the Ministry of Agriculture demanding reform, and in 1985 the International Monetary Fund was called in to help the economy.

The elections on 16 May 1986 were unique as the three candidates were all ex-presidents: Bosch, Majluta, and the man who won, Joaquín Balaguer, now blind, whose term of office took him past his 82nd birthday.

For more aspects of the country's history, see Samaná and Santo Domingo.

Warning. Avoid the big cities during election campaigns as many people believe that bullets influence the ballots.

INDUSTRY

The Dominican Republic's economy is basically agricultural, with thousands of small farmers working their own plots or renting from the large landowners. The broad fertile plains primarily grow sugar cane, with tobacco, rice and fruit as lesser crops. In the foothills and lower mountains, coffee and cacao (the basis of cocoa) are grown, with bananas, cassava and peanuts yielding important crops anywhere.

Sugar. Sugar has been the traditional mainstay of the country for generations; Diego Columbus, eldest son of Christopher and governor of the West Indies from 1509 to '23, introduced the cane to Hispaniola in 1493, and it remained the republic's highest earner until overtaken by tourism in recent years.

There are now 16 working mills in the country, 12 run by the State Sugar Council, the *Consejo Estatal de Azúcar*, or CEA. The cane-cutting season, *la zafra*, runs from November to June, in which time the mills are busy; in the *tiempo muerto*, the 'dead time,' they are overhauled.

The Dominican Republic produces about 1,200,000 tons of sugar a year, 75% of which goes to the USA; exports were worth US$133,800,000 in 1986, with raw coffee the next biggest foreign exchange earner at US$112,800,000. Cocoa beans, at US$58,800,000, were a long way behind, and raw tobacco exports were worth just US$18,500,000 in 1986.

Tourism. But tourism is now the biggest earner; in 1986 there were 25,000 stopover visitors plus 11,000 cruise visitors; in 1988 there were 800,000 tourists in total, bringing in US$600,000,000.

Industry's main products are animal feed, beer, cement, chocolate, glass, molasses, rum, sugar, textiles and vegetable oils.

Gold. Gold and nickel are mined in the Cordillera Central, with clay, gypsum, salt and bauxite coming from other parts of the country: they are exported as raw materials rather than as finished goods, the 1986 export value of gold and silver alloy being an impressive US$111,800,000.

Free zones. The country's eight 'free zones' now attract US and Korean light manufacturing and assembly industries, drawn by the tax-free status and the plentiful supply of cheap labour: minimum wages are RD$500 (US$80, £50) per *month*.

MAPS

There is virtually one moderately good map of the Dominican Republic on the world market, the *Mapa Turístico*. It can be bought, with difficulty, in Santo Domingo and the main tourist areas, and it is also available for £4.95 through Edward Stanford Ltd, 12-14 Long Acre, London, WC2E 9LP, ✆071.836.1321. and in the USA through Rand-McNally in New York, Chicago and San Fransisco.

The map has numerous small errors, particularly with roads around Higuey and the location of the national parks. It shows the country on a scale of 1:672,000, with no indication of contours and no hint that some of the routes it calls 'secondary roads' are passable only to four-wheel-drive trucks or trials bikes. If you're planning to use it on your exploration of the backwoods, (and what option do you have?) read this book first!

It has its good points; the town plans are good, and cover Santo Domingo, Santiago, Sosúa and Puerto Plata — and the key is in English.

In view of the problem, this book has more extensive maps than usual, locating every place mentioned in the text — which the *mapa turístico* certainly doesn't.

NEWSPAPERS

Of the many Spanish-language daily newspapers published in the country, the *Listín Diario* is reputed to be one of the best between here and Buenos Aires. No wonder; its staff trained with *El País* in Spain.

Other reasonable dailies are *Hoy*, *El Caribe*, *El Sol*, and the *Nuevo Diario*. Even if your Spanish is poor, these papers are convenient for finding what's on at the cinema.

English-language newspapers for tourists include the bi-weekly *Touring* and the weekly *Santo Domingo News*. Tourist magazines, available from the Ministry of Tourism, include *Bohío Dominicano* and *La Cotica;* the latter appears in many languages.

Foreign newspapers. English-language papers such as the *Miami Herald* are available in the big resorts but they are two days old and very expensive. *Time* and other US magazines are in many bookshops.

POLICE

The enforcers of the law, the *Policía Nacional*, are members of the armed forces and wear large white colonial-style hats and grey uniforms. When acting as traffic cops they sometimes stop people to check documents, but their usual response to tourists is to ask where they're from, shake hands, and wave them on.

You're unlikely to see a uniformed policeman except in the main streets of Santo Domingo. This doesn't mean the police are not there; they're in plain clothes. It's worth knowing that the uniformed police carry their guns and batons openly — but the secret police have theirs concealed.

My advice is to avoid the police as their job doesn't normally bring them into contact with tourists and their problems, and few speak English.

The special riot police, the *cascos negros* or black hats, are on call for raiding sleazy bars, to clear up trouble during anti-government demonstrations, and to keep a lookout for drugs.

Tourist police. In the Colonial City of Santo Domingo — the old heart of the capital — and the major tourist resorts, female tourist police are now on duty, but they appear to do nothing and they can't even speak English!

POPULATION

The estimated population of the Dominican Republic is 6,675,000, which gives an average density of 355 per square mile (137 per sq.km) and, despite an infant mortality rate of 6.5%, a growth rate of around 4.5% — which means there is a population boom in progress. For comparison, the UK has an average of 603 per square mile (233p.s.km.), Texas has 62p.s.m. (24p.s.km.), and Maryland 432p.s.m (167p.s.km.).

The early Spanish colonists killed most of the Amerind population, and so they brought in slaves from Jamaica and Haiti, descendants of original African slaves, to work the land.

Racial mix. Today, about 65% of the people are mulato (mixed black and white), 25% are white, and 10% are black. Freed slaves from USA's southern states migrated to the Samaná Peninsula in the mid-19th-cent, and a small group of European Jews settled near Puerto Plata in the early 1940s.

Get away from it all at Playa Grande near San Juan.

The largest city is Santo Domingo with a 1981 census population of 1,313,172, now put at between 1,500,000 and 2,000,000; other large towns are Santiago, 278,000 at the census; La Romana at 91,000; San Pedro de Macoris at 78,000; San Fransisco de Macoris at 65,000; Concepción La Vega (its full name) at 52,000; Barahona at 49,000 and Puerto Plata at 45,000.

Many Haitians live in the Dominican Republic, legally or illegally, and between 500,000 and 1,000,000 Dominicans live in the USA, many of them without residence status.

POSTAL SERVICE

The postal system is cheap, but it is also unreliable; you certainly cannot count on rapid delivery, either internally or externally. Look for the Spanish word *Correos*.

Postage rates: these postage rates for letters up to 19gm were valid in mid 1989:

USA, Canada, Central America, Caribbean; RD$0.50.

South America, Spain; RD$0.75.

All other European countries; RD$1.

Elsewhere; RD$1.50.

Stamps are on sale only at post offices, and the postal system is totally independent of the telephone system.

PUBLIC HOLIDAYS

Speaking with the authority of one who has worked in the Dominican Republic, the actual public holidays are:

January:	1	New Year's Day.
	6	Epifanía; Epiphany, or Three Kings Day.
	21	Nuestra Señora de Altagracia.
	26	Duarte's Day.
February:	27	Independence Day.
Good Friday.		
May:	1	Labour Day.
		Corpus Christi (not fixed, but around 25th).
August:	16	Restoration Day.
September:	24	Nuestra Señora de Mercedes, (Our Lady of Grace).
December:	25	Christmas Day.

You may see the following dates given in reference books, but I can testify they weren't public holidays for *me!*

April:	14	Pan-American Day.
July:	16	Foundation of Sociedad la Trinitaria.
October:	12	Columbus Day.
	24	United Nations Day.
November:	1	All Saints' Day.

Dominicans consider the Easter weekend to be their summer holiday, so native hotels of all types are full and increase their prices. Beaches are overcrowded with exhuberant Dominicans.

PUBLIC TOILETS (RESTROOMS)

There are no public toilets (restrooms) in the country. When the need arises you must use what's available in a restaurant or bar, and anticipate that conditions vary according to the establishment. Men should note that the concrete structure with water running into it is a urinal, not a wash-basin.

Ask for *el baño,* 'ell ban-yo,' which means 'the bathroom' and thereby shows the United States' influence. If presented with the choice of two doors, men should opt for *Caballeros* and women for *Damas.*

All hotels have European style toilet bowls, not the more primitive hole-in-the-floor effort, but only the smarter hotels provide paper. The open countryside has lush vegetation that will be even lusher after your visit.

RADIO and TELEVISION

Radio. The Dominican Republic has 179 radio stations broadcasting in AM and FM; the majority have an output relying very heavily on merengue, salsa or sports commentaries but among the exceptions are *Clásica 97FM* which offers classical music only and *HEJB 95.7FM* which has classical concerts at 1200-1400 and 2000-2200. Rock is available on *Radio Listín* on 99.5FM and *LA 91* on 91.1FM. Dominicans listen incessantly to merengue — and like it at high volume.

BBC and VOA. The Voice of America broadcasts in English on this schedule:

```
0000-0100 ...............  1580KHz, 6130KHz, 9455KHz, 11695KHz
1000-1200 ...............  1580KHz, 6030KHz, 6165KHz, 9590KHz.
```

BBC World Service reception suffers from local topography but you can try it daily on:

```
11,775MHz, 25,48m ...........................  1100-1330 (midday)
9,915MHz, 30.26m ...............................  2200-0430 (night)
7,325MHz, 40.96m ...............................  2200-0330 (night)
6,195MHz48.43m ...............................  1100-1330 (midday)
5.975MHz, 50.21m ...............................  2000-0430 (night)
.930MHz, 322.58m ...........................  00-0230, 1600-1615
```

Or you can tune in to Fidel Castro in Havana!

Television. This small and poor country has five national television channels, all of them transmitting the same mixture of programmes, from variety to news and baseball to soap operas (*telenovelas*);

Dominicans, the women in particular, love the soaps. All broadcasts are in Spanish.

English-language programmes are available to the wealthy Dominicans and are in most high-priced tourist hotels, by courtesy of US cable television beamed into Santo Domingo by satellite. Under ideal conditions your choice is from CNN, ESPN, MTV, VHI, CBS from Chicago, NBC from Atlanta, Channel 9 from New York, The Discovery Channel, HBO (Home Box Office), Cinemax, Showtime, The Disney Channel and Lifetime, but you will seldom have all available at once.

A few bars in the capital and the tourist areas also subscribe to cable television.

Package tourists might like to see Channel 30's 30-minute tourist-orientation film in their hotel. It's glossy, but shows some of the country's beauty spots.

RESIDENCE QUALIFICATIONS and BUYING PROPERTY

Many US and European citizens have bought property and started businesses in recent years in the Dominican Republic, with the government encouraging the foreign investment and removing all bureaucratic obstacles — but there is still much red tape to cut before you get a residence permit.

Property hunting? Property hunters should look in the *Santo Domingo News,* available in all tourist hotels, and call in at some of the realty offices (estate agencies) which have sprung up, particularly on the north coast.

Make absolutely certain you never buy property within 60 metres of the sea as this land belongs to the navy and cannot be in private ownership.

Investing? Potential investors in industry or tourism will find many sources of information in the capital, but first try the *Consejo Promotor de Inversiones Extranjeras,* the Foreign Investment Promotion Council, ✆(809)532.3281, −3286 and the Secretary of State for Tourism, ✆685.3029, 682.8181, −8189.

Moving in? After you've bought property, you'll want residential status. This is a time-consuming and frustrating process beginning with a call at the *Departamento de Emigración* in Santo Domingo with results of a blood test and a chest radiology, a letter of good conduct from your home country, a report from your doctor confirming your good health, and 15 photographs. You will also have your fingerprints taken.

Something more than a year later you should get your residence papers.

RESTROOMS see PUBLIC TOILETS

76

SPORTS

Baseball. The national sport, and the sport of the young, is baseball, not only as a means of releasing surplus energy but also as a possible highway to fame, fortune, and escape to North America where many Dominicans hold places in the big-league teams. Dominicans are indeed good players of this game which was borrowed from the Amerinds, and you'll see stadiums in every large town, as well as improvised pitches in every village, with amateur teams battling it out on Sunday afternoons.

There are five major national crowd-drawing teams for the October-to-late-January season, with games being held on any day of the week usually starting at 1600; look for posters announcing the next match.

Cock-fighting. Forgive me for including this cruel activity under 'sport,' but that's how Dominicans see it. They spend years developing a strain of cock, *gallo*, and put their birds in the ring at the age of 14 months, matching them with rivals of exactly equal weight, while the fights' followers wager large sums on the outcome.

Cock-fighting is a Sunday-afternoon activity, with cock pits to be found everywhere. The so-called 'sport' can be seen as an extension of the owner's libido and machismo, so emotions can run high; the contests last only a few minutes and can be bloody affairs. Cock-fighting is so ingrained that it generates its own vocabulary, similar to bull-fighting in Spain and cricket in England.

Cock-fighting is big business and draws large crowds. This fight is near Higuey.

Dominoes. Dominoes shares with cock-fighting the role of national obsession, but in the Dominican Republic it's played by two teams of two people, each person slapping his dominoes, *fichas,* down noisily and accusing his opponents of cheating. It's not a quiet game at all.

SPORTS FOR TOURISTS

If you carry a Professional Association of Diving Instructors card, then **scuba diving** is open to you in most resorts. No PADI card? You can train quickly at several schools, with my recommendation going to Leo and Linda's diving school in La Romana; see the section on this resort.

You can go **windsurfing** at almost every resort – Cabarete, east of Sosúa, claims to be the Dominican Republic's windsurfing capital – and there are numerous opportunities for **deep-sea fishing, horse-riding** and **tennis.**

The country is a **golf**ers' paradise, with some of the top courses designed by Pete Dye (he is responsible for the Teeth of the Dog in Casa de Campo) and Robert Trent Jones.

TELEPHONES

The Caribbean telephone system is partially integrated with that of the United States and Canada in that most islands, including the Dominican Republic, share the area code 809. Phoning from Santo Domingo to Los Angeles is no more an international call than is phoning Philadelphia (area code 215) from Baltimore (area code 301). The system differs from that in the USA by having far fewer telephone companies: the Dominican Republic offers the choice of **Codetel** and **DDD.**

CODETEL

The *Compañía Dominicana de Teléfonos,* Codetel (pronounced *co-deh-tel*), is a subsidiary of the American GTE corporation. It provides domestic phone links using a microwave network which also covers Puerto Rico and Haiti, and international links by satellite from the ground communications station at Cambita, near San Cristobal, as well as by submarine cable from Santo Domingo to the Virgin Islands and on to Jacksonville, Florida.

Local calls. In the major towns there are blue American-style public phone booths in the street. A call will cost about RD$0.25 to a number in the same town; phoning from hotels is more expensive.

International calls. There are two ways of making international calls: the easier is from a Codetel office (these offices are listed in the later chapters) where an English-Spanish bilingual operator asks for the number you're calling, then dials it for you. Person to person calls are accepted (*i.e.* your call is connected only to the person whom you've named). Finally, you pay at the counter in pesos or using any

The unacknowledged Dominican hero, the cane cutter, keeps the economy going.

major credit or charge card.

The difficult way is to dial the number yourself from a street booth, pushing in coins as fast as you can.

As the Codetel offices are located mainly for tourists' use you will almost certainly make your calls from them, but if you cannot reach an office these are the Codetel dialling codes you need:

To Caribbean islands within area code 809: 0 + 809 + subscriber's 7-digit number;

To USA and Canada: 0 + area code + subscriber's 7-digit number;

To Europe and elsewhere: 01 + country code + area code + subscriber's number. (*when dialling to the UK, omit the 0 in the area code*)

DDD

DDD means Direct Distance Dialing — yes, in English! — and is the state-run telephone system's overseas network, available in around 35 exchanges. The DDD system does not have operators so the caller must dial direct, as the name implies. As DDD doesn't have booths either, you are not likely to come into contact with it unless you phone from a business office, a non-tourist hotel or a private house.

These are the dialling codes you need, should you use DDD, and you will note they differ slightly from Codetel's:

79

To USA and Canada: 1 + area code + subscriber's 7-digit number.

To Europe and elsewhere: 011 + country code + area code + subscriber's number. (*when dialling to the UK, omit the 0 in the area code*)

   National codes. For dialling to Europe:

Belgium	32	France	33
Germany (West)	49	Italy	39
Netherlands	31	Spain	34
Sweden	46	Switzerland	41
United Kingdom	44		

TIME

   The Dominican Republic is on Atlantic Standard Time, which is one hour ahead of Eastern Standard Time (New York and Miami time) and four hours behind Greenwich Mean Time. There is no 'summer time' ('daylight saving time') in the republic: the clocks are never altered.

   In winter, dusk comes around 1800 to 1830 hrs, and in summer around 1930 to 200 hrs. It is always daylight by 0700. Twilight is brief.

WEIGHTS & MEASURES

   There is a great mixture of systems in use. The British Imperial system is used for weights, with 16 ounces to the pound (*16 onzas a la libra*). The metric equivalents are: 1 ounce = 28.350gm; 1 pound = 0.4536kg.

   The US gallon (*galón*) of 3.785 litres is used for liquids, such as petrol; Britons should remember the Imperial gallon is 1.2 US gallons, or 4.546 litres.

   The Imperial system is used for short measures, such as 1 yard (*yarda*), equal to 0.9144m.

   The metric system is used for long measures, with distances between towns given in kilometers. Metric measures are also used for land surfaces in cities: 1 sq m = 1.196 sq yds.

WHAT YOU WON'T LIKE

   The most shocking thing about the Dominican Republic is its poverty. Compared with Europeans and North Americans, the Dominicans are very poor, but you, the visitor, should try to adjust yourself a little to signs of poverty – after all, you can't do anything about it – without letting it threaten your contact with the people and their culture.

   Begging. Poverty is no crime in itself and doesn't make a good person bad, and it hasn't made this fun-loving race bitter or resentful. It may have more effect on you, particularly in Santo Domingo's poor areas and in the countryside. You will be affected by the begging

The beautiful north coast, looking west from Sosúa.

Sip a piña colada while enjoying this view from Sosúa's Sand Castle Hotel.

Cane workers go 'gaga' during Easter week throughout the rural areas of the Dominican Republic.

Amber! The Dominican Republic is one of the world's leading sources of this beautiful gem.

children, and find it hard not to feel guilty at your own obvious wealth. You will also find it difficult to understand how there can be so much contrast between the rich and the poor.

Your relative wealth may be a problem when dealing with local people as you may feel that some extend the hand of friendship not because of your radiant personality but because of your wallet. You will always be a gringo to these people.

Exploitation. You won't like the exploitation you see; of the Haitian men cutting cane for next to nothing; and of the Dominican women, so dominated by their own menfolk. An unaccompanied female tourist will find the Dominican male persistent in the pursuit of the object of his desire, and a wounded machismo is capable of making him say some unpleasant things if his advances are rejected. One cynical belief is that white women are AIDS carriers, and discontents are not above hissing "Sida!" at white girls. If it happens, ignore it.

Culture. You will also find the Dominican Republic a little bleak if your interest is in cultural activities, such as visiting museums and archaeological sites. The Dominican Republic is, above all, a fun place despite (or because of?) its poverty, a place where serious issues are often ignored. There will be times when this attitude can annoy, as when your guagua driver has had too much drink, or when you're searching for information on anything cultural, from buying a book to asking such mundane things as "When does the festival begin?"

Don't expect to have everything laid on once you're outside the tourist areas. Tourism is in its infancy and people don't understand the gringo sense of urgency.

Silence. If you like peace and quiet, you'll be amazed at how easily the Dominicans can destroy it. I remember being in a beautiful cave looking at the stalactites in perfect silence when a group of locals burst in with merengue music blaring. In non-tourist hotels merengue may often make sleep near impossible, for the Dominican interprets the need for silence as being upset or unwell, and there is always pressure on you to laugh, shout, and drink, *para compartir*.

A condominium is a block of apartments in which each is owned by its occupants.

12: WILDLIFE

Flora and fauna

THE DOMINICAN REPUBLIC is a tropical paradise – but with the inevitable blemishes caused by thoughtless mankind. There is much interesting wildlife on the land and in the sea, and there are still many unspoiled habitats in which to enjoy the natural world.

The sea

The waters of the Caribbean are crystal clear, giving perfect visibility for the snorkeller or scuba diver. Among the interesting creatures you will meet are the parrot fish, *pez loro;* the porcupine fish, *pez guanabana,* which when threatened swells to resemble a football with spikes; the slender trumpet fish; and many sub-species of angel and butterfly fish. These live on the coral reefs with the sponges, morays, lobsters, crabs, urchins, and other creatures.

Coral. There are many types of coral that create the reefs around the Dominican Republic, with the brain, staghorn, elkhorn and fire corals particularly distinguishable; the latter is particularly painful, too, if you touch it. The most beautiful is the sea fan, which is deep violet fading to white in its extremities, and as delicate as lace. The reefs are in shallow water and within easy swimming distance of the beach, and they circle most of the coastline. *For the sake of conservation in a land that hasn't yet thought much on 'green' issues, don't damage the reef in any way.*

Sharks and others. Among the larger inhabitants of the inshore waters are green, leatherback and hawksbill turtles, all of them increasingly rare because of hunting by man for their meat and their decorative shells. *You should avoid buying anything derived from the turtle, notably shell in souvenir shops and turtle-meat in restaurants.*

Sharks are not a hazard at all in the shallower inshore waters; for example, the only shark attack in memory at Key West Memorial Hospital in Florida is a minor incident in 1983. *El tiburón* prefers the deeper waters, particularly the Mona Passage, where he can be a menace to fishermen, and to those luckless people aspiring to be Dominican-Yorks.

The dangerous species are the mako, tiger and hammerhead, and they can give you a very nasty fright if you go spearfishing in deep water; trail your catch on a long line well away from you, or put the fish in your boat as soon as possible, for sharks are sensitive to the movement of injured fish and to the smell of blood – some scientists believe sharks can also detect electro-magnetic impulses from a fish in pain.

Sport fishing. The larger fish of the open sea, such as marlin, tuna (which travel in schools and can reach speeds of up to 35mph (55kph)), and dolphin-fish (no relation at all to the dolphin mammal), all make good eating and are thus targets for the sport fisherman, most of whom come down from the United States.

Beauty at sea. A beautiful and common sight in a small boat out at sea is the flying fish, which are only around nine inches (25cm) long yet can glide at 35mph (55kph) for up to 750ft (250m), staying airborne for as much as 15 seconds. And in February and March you can see humpback whales – ballenas jorobadas – in Samaná Bay where they congregate to feed.

The land

Among the exotic land creatures of the Dominican Republic are iguanas and crocodiles – the latter known to the locals as *caimanes* although they are not caymans by the English definition. You can find crocs if you hire a boat to Isla Cabritos in Lago Enriquillo; for the iguanas you'll need to rough it to Pedernales (both roads into the town are deplorably bad) and take a boat along the coast.

More accessible creatures include the many lizards that come in all shapes, sizes and colours, the big land crabs (*cangrejos*) which are delicious to eat, the fist-sized, slow-moving, hairy-legged spiders popularly known as tarantulas, and the myriad beautiful butterflies and birds.

Butterflies. There are 151 species of butterflies found in Hispaniola, 41 of which are unique to the island. The monarch and the several species of swallowtail are particularly colourful.

Birds. Hispaniola is rich in resident and migratory birdlife, with more than 20 species unique to the island, but habitat destruction and relentless hunting, particularly in Haiti, are putting pressures on the population.

Around the coasts look for the brown pelican, *el pelícano, el alcatraz;* royal tern, *la gaviota real;* and the magnificent frigatebird, *tijereta,* (the name means 'earwig' in Spain), a pirate of the seas. By riverbanks look for the green heron, *el cracrá, el cuaco;* in Lake Enriquillo and near Montecristi in the north-west look for the roseate flamingo, *el flamenco,* the bird which gave its name to a dance; and in freshwater rivers as well as along the coast, watch for the belted kingfisher, *el martín pescador,* and the osprey, *el guincho.*

The turkey vulture, *el aura tiñosa*, and the American kestrel, *la cuyaya, el cernícalo*, are widespread birds of prey inland. The cattle egret, *la garza ganadera*, feeds on lizards, frogs and insects in pastureland, and forms large flocks at dawn and dusk flying to and from its mangrove roosts.

In the lowlands look for the grey kingbird, *el pestigre*, and other flycatchers, and the northern mockingbird, *el ruiseñor*, (the name means 'nightingale' in Spain); the latter has a melodious song which has made it Florida's state emblem. Lowland birds also include the common ground dove, *la rolita;* smooth-billed ani, *el judío*, (the 'Jew'), and four other cuckoo types: the mangrove, yellow-billed, bay-breasted and Hispaniola lizard cuckoos − *pájaros bobos* all.

Smaller birds include the bananaquit, *la cigüita;* and three hummingbirds, the Antillean mango, *el zumbador grande;* the Hispaniola emerald, *el zumbador*, mostly found in higher locations; and the vervain hummingbird, *el zumbadorcito*, the second-smallest bird in the world and frequently mistaken for an insect.

Other exotics are the palmchat, *la cigüa palmera*, which has large communal nests; the Antillean palm swift, *el vencejo chiquito;* the Hispaniolan parrot, *el perico*, more frequently seen as a cage-bird but now enjoying some protection; the common and noisy Hispaniolan *woodpecker, el carpintero;* and the village weaver, *la madam sagá, la cigüa Haitiana*.

Bird books. For further information on Hispaniolan birdlife read James Bond's *The Birds of the West Indies*, (Collins, London), £8.95, although a good supplement, especially for more comprehensive illustrations, is Roger Peterson's *Eastern Birds − A Field Guide to the Birds of Eastern and Central North America*, (Houghton Mifflin, Boston, MA, $12.95).

Spanish speakers will find Annabelle Stockton de Dod's *Aves de la República Dominicana* useful, but its illustrations are limited.

National parks. Many of these creatures, plus a wealth of trees and other plants, can be seen in their unspoiled state in the country's five national parks. As they are all in remote areas, visitors must be prepared to live rough, and should expect adventure rather than comfort; there is little organisation, but to get the most from a park visit you should hire a guide either at the park entrance or at the nearest village; his fee should be modest.

The parks are:

Amando Bermúdez and **J. del Carmen Ramírez** in the Cordillera Central.

Isla Cabritos in Lago Enriquillo.

Los Haitises on the south of Samaná Bay.

El Parque Nacional del Este south-east of La Romana and including

Isla Saona.

Pay no attention to the 'national park' symbol on the *Mapa Turístico*, as its information is wrong.

Tour company. The local tour operator Maritisant, of C/ Duarte 12, Esq. Padre Billini, Santo Domingo, ✆685.7910, organises excursions to Haitises — and to Saona Island off the south-east tip of the country — and as I write is planning to extend its services to Lago Enriquillo.

The Flora: trees. The Dominican Republic is outstanding for the variety and grace of its trees. Flowering trees include the noticeable African tulip tree; the pink cassia; and the best-known of them all, the poinciana or flame tree, which turns brilliant red during the May-to-July flowering season. Other specimens that remind you this is the tropics are the baobab, the banana, the cacao which gives us cocoa, the mango, and the beautiful palms including the coconut, the royal and the traveller's palm, which spreads out like a vast fan.

Flowers. Dominicans love to have their houses surrounded by beautiful flowers, with a wide range from which to choose. Among the exotics are the angel's trumpet, the bird of paradise flower, bougainvillea, monkey tail, and perhaps the best-known, the hibiscus, which seems to have been designed to set off the girls' ebony-black hair.

Mangroves. The mangrove swamps found in many places in the Dominican Republic support their own unique ecosystems of interdependent organisms. The cattle egret, blue heron and vulture, roost and nest in the upper branches; spiders, dragonflies, and other insects operate in the lower branches. Lizards and crabs live in or just above the mud, venturing higher to prey on the insect life, while in the tidal zones are oysters and many species of fish adapted to this environment.

The middle of a mangrove swamp has a peace and silence that is very special — particularly so in a land where noise often reigns supreme.

STOP! The Spanish word *PARE,* pronounced 'parray,' appears on signs at road junctions. It means *STOP.*

DISCOVER THE
DOMINICAN REPUBLIC

THE DOMINICAN REPUBLIC divides naturally into distinct regions: the north coast including the Samaná peninsula; the Cibao and the Central Highlands; Santo Domingo and Boca Chica; the east, from San Pedro de Macoris; and the south-west, known locally as the south. We'll discover the country in that order.

Hotel pricing. Hotel prices increase and currencies fluctuate, so I have given the hotels and restaurants a dollar-rating to indicate price group rather than an exact price, which is for a *standard room with double bed, per night, with tax, in high season,* (low season is much cheaper), and *a full meal including drinks.*

HOTELS				
Dollar-rating	my rating	Dominican pesos	US dollars	pounds sterling
1$	very cheap	10 — 40	1.60 — 6.40	1 — 4
2$	cheap	40 — 80	6.40 — 12.80	4 — 8
3$	cheap-mod	80 — 150	12.80 — 24	8 — 15
4$	moderate	150 — 300	24 — 48	15 — 24
5$	mod-expensive	300 — 600	48 — 96	30 — 60
6$	expensive	600 — 1,000	96 — 160	60 — 100
7$	very expensive	>1,000	>160	>100

RESTAURANTS				
2$	cheap	25 — 50	4 — 8	2.50 — 5
4$	moderate	50 — 100	8 — 16	5 — 10
6$	expensive	100 — 200	16 — 32	10 — 20
7$	very expensive	>200	>32	>20

OTHER SYMBOLS

In Chapters 13 to 17, these symbols are used: ❶ — tourist office or other information point. ➋ — bus or other public transport stand on a town map. ✕ — restaurant available in a hotel; also location of a restaurant on a town map. ⌂ — watersports available. ⌁ — boating or boat hire available.

AC — air-conditioning ('fan' in text means a ceiling fan).

P — parking for car or motor-cycle on the premises.

13: THE NORTH COAST

The Amber Coast

THE NORTH COAST stretches from Monte Cristi by the Haitian frontier to the eastern tip of the breathtakingly-beautiful Samaná peninsula, and includes the popular tourist resorts of Puerto Plata, Playa Dorada and Sosúa, as well as several lesser-known hideaways.

This is the major tourist area of the Dominican Republic, catering principally in winter for Canadians who fly from Montreal and Toronto to Puerto Plata Airport. Puerto Plata, the main town, is in the middle of the coastline and has dominated this Amber Coast since shortly after Christopher Columbus's arrival.

Summary. West lies **Monte Cristi,** devoid of tourism and tourist interest; then comes the crowded beach of **Luperón** with a huge hotel beside the sands, yet with difficult access. Finally there is **Cofresí,** well worth a visit for its relative solitude.

Costambar's beach is a little less impressive but, because Puerto Plata is only a few miles away, is more expensive.

Puerto Plata is a pretty town dominated by the mountain of Isabel de Torres, 2,602ft (793m) high, its splendid summit garden accessible by cable car.

East of the town, **Long Beach** runs into Marapica and on to **Playa Dorada** with its big, self-contained hotel complex. The 'golden beach' is not the most beautiful in the country, and its waters are not crystal clear, but it is a highly developed tourist area convenient for the airport and the town.

Further east lies the twin community of **Sosúa,** the Dominican part, Charamicos, on the western end of the beach and the European part, El Batey, at the east. These excellent sands, ideal for the sun-and-fun visitor, lie in a beautiful crescent-shaped bay, and the town is a meeting point for Dominicans and tourists — which means you must expect the locals to try selling you their craft products. Sosúa is not the place for those tourists looking for peace and quiet.

East, again, is the rapidly-developing **Cabarete,** host to the 1987 Windsurfing World Championships. The splendid long beach has a back-up of cheap hostels and rooms for renting, and is much less congested than Sosúa.

Then comes **Río San Juan,** a pleasant little town with a small lagoon known as *Laguna Gri-Gri,* whose qualities have been somewhat exaggerated in some travel brochures. But east of here lie the Dominican Republic's really beautiful beaches which extend to the Samaná peninsula, broken only by **Nagua,** a rather disappointing town without a beach.

The beaches of **Playa Grande** and **La Preciosa** are just as nature created them − but that also means there are no hotels in the area.

Cabrera is nothing special, but its beaches are once more in the first category: try the sands of Cabo Francés Viejo two miles (3km) west, and those at La Entrada, seven miles (10km) east. The sands around **Nagua** tend to be dirty as the brown river waters circulate in the bay, but pristine conditions begin again seven miles (10km) further east.

The road. The road along the Amber Coast is bad east from Cabarete, with large holes and stretches without tarmac. Between Cabarete and Puerto Plata there have been attempts at improvement, while the road over the Cordillera Septentrional from Puerto Plata, and the 72-mile (117-km) main route from Santiago to Monte Cristi, are excellent.

MONTE CRISTI

Lying in the north-west corner of the Dominican Republic is the quiet and somewhat sleepy town of Monte Cristi, whose old world charm reflects its more prosperous past; some of the timber-frame houses were prefabricated in France and shipped out, with all their furniture.

The countryside is flat and dry, suitable only for herding goats, and the most obvious industry is salt production, by mining and by evaporation in the salt pans.

Beaches. Three miles (5km) to the north is a thin strip of sand totally without shade, but the sea is clear and shallow. If you rent a boat you may be ferried to Cayo Cabrito, a tiny island with a beach, called Isla Cabra on the official map. Beyond the mountainous headland of El Morro the coast is more rugged and interesting, with an attractive beach − but access is difficult.

Birds. The area around Monte Cristi and the sheltered Bay of Manzanillo, by the Haitian border, are good spots for watching the many migratory birds.

Hotel:

Hotel Chico, near the town centre; clean; fan or AC; ✕; night-watchman for vehicles. 2$.

The cable car makes a spectacular ascent of Isabel de Torres.

PUNTA RUCIA

You're looking for tropical paradise? The beautiful beach of Punta Rucia is midway between Monte Cristi and Puerto Plata, but is far from the beaten track. Access is either from the Santiago-Monte Cristi road by turning north at Villa Elisa for Estero Hondo: the track is rough but passable for larger vehicles – or by driving west from Luperón, past the archaeological site of La Isabela, crossing the Bajabonica river and going through Villa Isabela; the point is 7½ miles (12km) further.

Christopher Columbus. La Isabela is where Columbus built his first settlement on the island of Hispaniola, historically of major importance but visually nothing more than an archaeological dig amid splendid country.

Hotel:

La Orquidea del Sol, on the beach, ✆581.5656; 24 rooms with 2 or 3 beds; rustic; AC; ✗; ⇌; ✦ to secluded bays and mangrove lagoon; 6$, but price is all-in. The area is famed for its wild orchids growing on the branches of decaying trees, hence the hotel's name.

LUPERON

Turn off the Puerto Plata-Santiago main road near Imbert, and travel west for 18 miles (30km) along a not-too-badly potholed road which meanders past gentle hills and quiet villages amid green and beautiful countryside.

Ciudad Marina Beach Resort. Luperón is a scruffy town but two miles (3km) further, the two-mile-long beach has the Ciudad Marina Beach Resort, ✆581.6262, −4153 (for more information ✆541.4341−43 in Santo Domingo). This large new complex has no connection with the village of Luperón except for using the beautiful Luperón Bay as a natural marina. The resort has excellent golden sand with deep clean water, a tennis village, an equestrian centre, an 18-hole golf course, and several hotels and condominiums which make it an attractive vacation area only one hour from Puerto Plata's international airport. The resort is managed by Dominicana de Hoteles, S.A, (Domitel), which also arranges sales of condos.

Hotels:

Luperón Beach Resort, at Ciudad Marina; ✆581.4153.

160 rooms with plans to expand to 310 and 188 suites. Large pool by ✗ (2$); hotel 6$. For a luxury stay on an excellent beach, this is unbeatable in the Puerto Plata area − but there is no infrastructure. Motor-cycles for hire, but I wonder where the guests can go?

Las Tres Hermanas, on approach to Luperón; 1$.

COFRESI

A locally-famous buccaneer has his name perpetuated in this mile-long beach, four miles (6km) west of Puerto Plata. There is no reef, so the water is deep enough for swimming near the coast, making it an ideal site for the only hotel in this quiet enclave.

Hotel:

Cofresí Beach Club Hotel, on promontory; built highrise on hillside, giving splendid views; ✗ Corsario and ✗ Sombrero. Recreation and activities area separate and lower; cliff-top disco, 2 pools, lagoon, fitness centre, 2 tennis courts. Full-board tariff with free drinks, 4$.

COSTAMBAR

Costambar is a fairly large tourist development two miles (3km) west of Puerto Plata, with private and rented condos and villas; for seekers of independence and intimacy it's a peaceful and pleasant alternative to the big hotels of Playa Dorada.

Here are shops, car- and moped-rental agencies, restaurants, sports facilities that include a semi-olympic pool, the 9-hole golf course of Los Mangos, tennis, and water-sports.

Apart-hotel:

Las Caobas, ✆562.4171, −7461.

Reservations through Dimargo in Santo Domingo. 40 fully-furnished rooms; 60 meters to beach; 4$.

Agency:

Atlantis, ✆586.3828; PO Box 684. Arranges rentals of apartments and villas for 2 or 4 people; each apartment has living room, bedroom(s), kitchen, bathroom; electricity by national grid, liable to failure. 4$.

PUERTO PLATA

Puerto Plata was founded by Frey Nicolás de Ovando in 1502 on the instructions of Christopher Columbus who had landed in the New World just 10 years earlier, and by 1577 the *Fortaleza de San Felipe*, St Philip's Fortress, had been built on what is now the extreme western end of the Malecón. It houses a small museum and is open daily, except Thurs, 0900-1200, 1500-1700 for RD$5.

The town commemorates its former wealth in its name, *plata* meaning not only silver but money as well – but you may find some people who argue that the silver is still there today, in the colour of the sea at sunset.

Amber Museum. Puerto Plata has always been a rival to Santo Domingo, standing so close to La Isabela, Columbus's settlement, and it's only in the present century that the capital has grown out of control, leaving the 'silver port' as a charming town of around 60,000 people and the undisputed capital of the country's amber coast; the Amber Museum is at the corner of Duarte and Villanueva near the central square, displaying pieces of amber up to 50 million years old, many with insects or small animals embedded. Mon-Sat, 0900-1600, RD$3.

Rum Factory. Another attraction, the Brugal Rum Factory, is on Av Colón between Duarte and Beller; tours Mon-Fri 0900-1200, 1400-1700, free – and you get a free sample.

The town itself has fine examples of Victorian wooden houses, many now beautifully maintanied in gingerbread-style and serving as gift shops or restaurants for the tourists.

With the blue sea on one side and the towering green bulk of Isabel de Torres on the other, Puerto Plata is one of my favourite towns in the country; nightlife is vibrant, daylife is relaxed, and the local people are courteous and friendly, accustomed to the tourists but not prone to hassling.

Isabel de Torres. The mountain of Isabel de Torres rises to 2,602 feet (793m), with a statue of Christ, a cafetería, and a small garden on the summit, from where there is a superb view. The cable car, *teleférico*, operates from a base off the road to Santiago (see town map) daily except Wed, 0800-1700, for RD$5 adults and RD$3 children. The service is often suspended in low season so check first.

Cupey. Behind the mountain lies the little town of Cupey, accessible only by trials bike along an extremely tough track from the

PUERTO PLATA

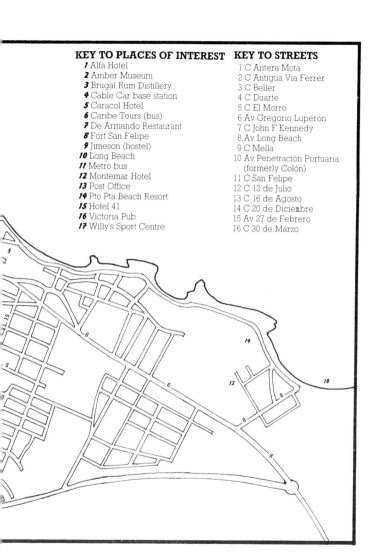

KEY TO PLACES OF INTEREST

1 Alfa Hotel
2 Amber Museum
3 Brugal Rum Distillery
4 Cable Car base station
5 Caracol Hotel
6 Caribe Tours (bus)
7 De Armando Restaurant
8 Fort San Felipe
9 Jimeson (hostel)
10 Long Beach
11 Metro bus
12 Montemar Hotel
13 Post Office
14 Pto Pta Beach Resort
15 Hotel 41
16 Victoria Pub
17 Willy's Sport Centre

KEY TO STREETS

1 C Antera Mota
2 C Antigua Via Ferrer
3 C Beller
4 C Duarte
5 C El Morro
6 Av Gregorio Luperón
7 C John F Kennedy
8 Av Long Beach
9 C Mella
10 Av Penetración Portuaria
   (formerly Colón)
11 C San Felipe
12 C 12 de Julio
13 C 16 de Agosto
14 C 20 de Diciembre
15 Av 27 de Febrero
16 C 30 de Marzo

Santiago road out of Puerto Plata; the track also takes you nearly to the summit of Isabel de Torres.

Puerto Plata has an excellent three-mile (5-km) Malecón, also known as the Circunvalación Norte, stretching from the fort in the west to Long Beach in the east; in the centre of town is a square whose wooden bandstand glows under green lights at night, giving the area a magical air.

Beaches. Long Beach, beginning at the eastern end of the Malecéon, is not in the top grade but it will do for sunbathing; the reef, some 70 meters away, makes the inshore waters too shallow for swimming, but three miles (5km) east is Playa Dorada, described below.

Plaza Turisol. The road takes you by Plaza Turisol, a modern shopping centre with restaurant and tourist amenities, including a shop for sub-aqua divers.

Two cruise ships a week, on average, call at Puerto Plata, and more than half the charter airliners use La Unión Airport, only a few minutes away, putting this resort firmly in the international class.

Hotels in Puerto Plata (a selection):

Puerto Plata Beach Resort, Av Malecón (east); ℂ586.4243, telex ITT.346.2027.

24 rooms, 192 suites; colour TV and US cable TV. Top quality, efficient and welcoming; central pool, casino, programmed activities, access to most organised tours of the Amber Coast. Across Malecón is small private beach; above is ✕ El Neptuno, good view and famed for seafood. 5$.

Hotel Montemar, near Long Beach; ℂ586.2800, telex ITT.346.2019.

104 rooms including 3 suites, 3 bungalows. Pool, ✕ La Isabela, disco Los Cocos, tennis, ⌫ at Marapica Beach, access by hotel's minibus. 4$.

Hotel Caracol, on Malecón, ℂ586.2588.

34 rooms with AC and TV; pool, ✕ El Caracol, night-club. 4$.

Hostal Jimeson, C/ John Kennedy (near main square), ℂ586.2177, – 4542.

22 rooms with AC and private bathrooms. Clean, quiet, yet in town centre. Reliable electricity and hot water. Well maintained wooden house, extended; reputable and recommended; lobby has collection of clocks. Street parking with night watchman. 4$.

Hotel Alfa, Padre Castellanos 20; ℂ586.2684.

10 rooms in clean, family-type hotel. Hot water, fan, P for motor-cycle. 2$.

Hotel 41, in poor part of town, near port; used for one-night or several-hour stands by locals but is clean and pleasant. Each room has private bathroom, water in bucket when mains off; fan. 2$.

There are numerous *pensiones* in town, from 1$ to 2$.

If you want to buy some Dominican jewellery you should take a look in the Amber Museum in Puerto Plata.

Restaurants, a selection from the 30 or more in town:

Dominican Joe's, C/ Beller 60, ✆586.1277. Owner is from Boston but the food is Dominican; tastefully restored turn-of-century house; open lunch, dinner, to 2400. 6$.

Victorian Pub, C/ Separación 9, ✆586.4240; elegant but informal atmosphere in beautiful gingerbread house with good garden; continental dishes; open 1100-2300. 6$.

Jimmy's Restaurant, C/ Beller 72, ✆586.4325; wide range of seafoods; in converted Victorian house, informal; musicians; candles on tables at night; 1100-2400. 6$.

De Armando, C/ Separación – C/ Antera Mota, ✆586.3418; national and international dishes with seafood specialities. 6$.

Austrian Restaurant Margarita, C/ Diagonal 11, ✆586.4030; special-ises in Austrian food served in a private home; good food and family atmosphere. Reserve by phone 1500-1600; meals from 1800. 4$.

La Palma Austria, C/ Presidente Vasquez 1, ✆586.4265; European cuisine; barbecue special on Friday; in smart restored house; 1800-2300. 4$.

Willy's Sport Centre Restaurant, Malecón, west end; informal, modern; Dominican and international cuisine; ample helpings; cable TV. 4$.

Parque Costero, Long Beach, ✆586.3577; large bohio restaurant serving inexpensive food; useful if spending day on beach; also open evenings. 4$.

Café Gallerie, C/ Separación 19, opposite Metro bus stn; opens early for breakfast but service can be slow. 4$.

Ice Cream Parlor, on main square; Helados Italianos 'Perugina;' have a sundae for RD$5.50 − a must!

Nightlife. Puerto Plata is fairly lively; the big hotels have their own discos and night clubs, but there is other entertainment in town, notably Vivaldi Studio near Long Beach (RD$15 entry). The central square is where everyone meets; failing that there is the Malecón which normally has merengue music blasting forth. The red light district, which looks like the set for a western film, has places such as the Don Mendez House of Pleasure.

There is also a baseball stadium on the road out to Sosúa.

Transport:

Buses. Metro and Caribe Tours both operate between Puerto Plata and Santo Domingo; Metro is at Separación − Salomé Ureña, ✆586.2825; Caribe is at 12 de Julio − José C. Ariza, ✆586.4544. Metro's fare to Sto Dgo is RD$30, to Santiago is RD$20 and to La Vega RD$12; see Chap 7 for timetable.

Guaguas. For Santiago catch the guagua in the barrio (quarter) La Javilla; for Sosúa and east go to the Malecón or the main road east. Sample fares; to Sosúa RD$2, Cabarete RD$3, Río San Juan, RD$6, Nagua RD$10, Samaná RD$15.

Taxis. Taxis of the *Sindicato de Chóferes Puerto Aéreo y Marítimo.* leave from C/ 12 de Julio 69, ✆586.3454. Fare to airport (US$9.60, £6).

The 'B' buses. Buses recognisable from the big 'B' on the front, follow a set route around town, along the Malecón to Playa Dorada, and return. Fare RD$0.50; service from 0600 to 1800; get on and off where you please.

Motoconchos. There is no shortage of motoconchos. Fares are RD$1 for the town, RD$2 Costambar and Playa Dorada entrance, RD$3 Cofresí; after 2200 add RD$1.

Car and motor-cycle rental. See Chap 7.

Tour Operators. Puerto Plata Tours, C/ Beller 70, ✆586.3858. Local tours.

Servicio Turístico Dominicano, Plaza Turisol, ✆586.5204, −5283. Selection of 15 tours from a visit to a tobacco factory to an all-sights tour of Santo Domingo costing US$32 per person.

Festivals: the main celebrations are the Amber Festival in the second week of October and *Patronales* (patron saints − San Felipe in this instance) on 5 July.

Post Office: On corner of Separación and 12 de Julio; Mon-Sat 0800-1700.

Locals relax near the bandstand in the colourful central park of Puerto Plata.

Eurotel at Playa Dorada has all the ingredients of a perfect holiday — including a view of Isabel de Torres mountain.

The Atlantic Coast has a rugged beauty that is not found on the Caribbean shores.

The lush Cibao valley stretches across much of the north.

Telephones: Codetel is at C/ Beller 58 and the airport.

Airline reservations: at Puerto Plata Airport:
Air Canada, ✆586.0252   American, ✆586.0325
Dominican, ✆586.0217   Pan Am ✆586.0227.

Medical assistance: 24 hours — Clínica Bournigal on C/ Antera Mota, a small hospital with intensive care ward.

24-hour pharmacy — Farmacia Deleite, J.F. Kennedy near Parque Luperón.

PLAYA DORADA

Here is the home of the big luxury resort hotel, such as you would find at Miami Beach or Palm Beach in Florida, on Spain's Costa del Sol, or at Nice on the French Riviera. Yet the Playa Dorada Beach Hotel Complex covers a mere 250 acres (1 sq km) in an enclosure built along the 2½ miles (4km) of Playa Dorada — 'golden beach.'

Three miles (5km) east of Puerto Plata and 10 minutes from the aiport. Playa Dorada aims to offer the ideal luxury vacation for sunstarved North Americans, and is now catering for Europeans as well.

As I write there are nine big luxury hotels in operation with three more under construction; until the commercial complex is completed, guests go into Puerto Plata to shop.

Golf. The 18-hole golf course designed by Robert Trent Jones runs through the complex, with all hotels having access.

Beach. Most hotels have their own private stretch of beach regardless of whether they front the sands; the remainder of the *playa dorada* is open to the public, including the day visitors from Puerto Plata. The beach is reasonable but not among the country's best; the water doesn't have the crystal clarity that you can find at Samaná, but it's deep enough for inshore swimming and a fringe of trees provides adequate shade.

Access to the public sands is just before the Jade Garden Restaurant from where the road leads down to a car park on the landward side of Donald's Beach Restaurant; walk through or around Donald's bohio-type establishment to reach the beach.

Atmosphere. This is a laid-back resort, marketed at the mature vacationer with a comfortably filled wallet who would rather relax on the sands or play golf than go searching for night life and excitement. If you want adventure, go on one of the day tours or hire some transport.

Prices are in the upper range, but most hotels quote tariffs which include full board, drinks and activities — the latter mainly confined to minibus services into Sosúa and Puerto Plata. There is also a radical difference between high and low season rates, winter being the most expensive when the North Americans escape their own cold climates, but with more Europeans coming in the summer low season there may soon be less of a differential.

Hotels:

Eurotel, ✆586.4333, −3663 (or Sto. Dgo. 567.5697); telex ITT.346.2033.

402 rooms in AC suites, studios and apartments. The hotel design is magnificent, from a tropical open-air lobby with mock jungle pool, to a central swim pool feeding a river, to beachfront restaurant, all giving an air of fantasy. Three ✗, bars, conference centre holding 600 people; regular evening shows, recently-added casino; ☎, tennis, golf, riding. Hire cycle or scooter to get into Puerto Plata. Tariff 4$ to 6$ depending which plan you buy, CP (Continental), Modified American (MAP) or Full American (FAP).

Jack Tar Village, ✆586.3800 (for information, 527.9299); telex ITT.346.2025.

300 rooms in AC apartments with cable TV. This was the first hotel in the complex, built in 1980; casino now extended to be what is claimed the country's biggest; gourmet ✗. Employs 750 locals. Hotel specialises in all-inclusive packages hence tariff is 6$.

Heavens, ✆586.5250, −4739.

150 AC rooms and suites with cable TV. Completed 1989, offering Olympic-size pool, full sports, ✗ Italiano. All-inclusive, 6$.

Dorado Naco, ✆586.2019, telex ITT.346.0554.

150 one- or two-bed AC apartments with kitchenettes, giving 202 rooms; cable TV. Sophisticated; full range of sports; ✗ Flamingo; a short walk from beach. 6$.

Villas Doras, ✆586.3000 (from USA 1.800.332.4872); telex ITT.346.2031, −0528.

172 rooms, 32 suites, 5 villa-cabins; AC, cable TV. Design is simple but tasteful; most sports; ✗ El Melao and ✗ Jardín de Jade. Footbridge over lagoon to beach. Probably the least expensive in complex, 5$.

Playa Dorada, ✆586.3988; telex ITT.346.2030.

254 rooms and suites with AC and cable TV; hotel is beside beach and has pool area; several ✗ and convention facilities; all regular sports. This is a complete resort-hotel. Tariff, high season, 7$, low season 5$.

Village Caraibe, ✆586.4811, reservations ✆(809)586.1101; telex ITT.346.2018.

184 rooms and suites with AC and TV. This hotel bills itself as a tennis, golf and beach resort; has 4 clay courts, use of golf course, and beach is short walk away. Many other sports. ✗ El Bohio Criollo. 5$.

Radisson, ✆586.5350 (from USA and Canada 800.333.3333).

336 rooms in fully-equipped apartments or two-bed villas with kitchenette, AC and TV. This hotel is for tennis players and has 7 top quality courts; for other sporting guests it offers a fitness centre, gymnasium, and all regular sports — but the beach is a little way off. Pool, ✗ La Condesa, and full convention facilities. 5$.

Victoria Resort, ✆586.4862, (reservations from USA ✆212.832.2277 or 800.223.6510; from Canada ✆800.424.5500).

120 rooms and suites with AC and private balconies set in personalised hotel with rustic architectural style on island in lagoon surrounded by golf course. Pool. Quiet sophistication. 6$.

Puerto Plata Village.

Not yet open; 488 rooms in two-room apartments or three-room villas. Two ✗, pool, in mock-village setting. Planned as a complete resort-hotel.

The Tropicana and the Flamenco will also open soon.

SOSUA

Of all the towns in the Dominican Republic, Sosúa feels the most European, and there is a certain buzz of excitement in the air. This is the resort for young people who want to meet other young people in a relaxed atmosphere; it is also the place to come if you want to meet the locals at work and play, for in Sosúa more than elsewhere the tourists and the islanders share the beach. The disadvantage is, of course, that the Dominicans will urge you to buy their oysters, coconuts or jewellery, and buskers will serenade you for a peso or two.

Sosúa — stress the accented vowel as in all Spanish words — is a lively and intimate town in two parts: El Batey is the tourist area to the east of the main bay, while Charamicos is the native area on the west; behind them both rises a hill giving a splendid panorama.

El Batey. El Batey is a resort of small hotels, guest houses, and tourist facilities ranging from discos, bars and steak houses to auto-rental agencies, with the beach never far away. The streets are crowded with a polyglot of nationalities, in the middle of which the locals are plying their wares and services: many visitors have their hair plaited and beaded by Haitian women. But beware — prices are rising as tourism makes its impact.

Charamicos. By contrast, Charamicos is squalid, but a lot cheaper. Come here if you're looking for bargain-basement accommodation or local colour, but lone girls seeking a room in Charamicos should remember that the path from El Batey runs beside the beach and they should be careful after dark; I wouldn't call the area dangerous, but petty theft is one of the corrupting results of tourism.

The larger hotels are sited higher above the bay, having the advantage of better views and cooling breezes, but the disadvantage of distance and a steep climb. The hoteliers have found the answer in a minibus shuttle service.

Jews. Sosúa owes its original prosperity to several hundred Jewish refugees who migrated here in the 1940s and established the dairy and meat industry which is still important today — and which explains not only the European atmosphere but also the synagogue near the small beach of La Playita.

Sports. The resort offers pedalos, windsurfing, snorkelling along the shallow coral reef, water-skiing, and cruising in a glass-bottomed boat. Onshore sport is the Sosúa Mini golf course, on the main road opposite El Batey's supermarket, open 0830-2400.

Hotels:

Between Puerto Plata and Sosúa:

Costa del Mar. In Cangrejo village, midway between the towns and 2km from airport. The Canadian woman owner has created a refreshing change from the huge hotels of Playa Dorada; the 16 rooms have twin double beds; small pool; own generator; van service to airport, Sosúa and beach (2km); independent travellers welcome. P, ✗, 3$.

Sand Castle, at Puerto Chiquito, ✆571.2420, 535.2601.

240 rooms, AC, in a beautiful hotel 2km from Charamicos; splendid view of village and of beach directly below; clifftop pool; 3 ✗; scooter rental — Sosúa is 5 mins. 5$.

In Charamicos:

There are several basic and cheap hotels in Charamicos, owned by Dominican families, including **Los Hermanitos, Hotel Taino** and **Hotel del Castillo** which is at C/ V. Gell 75. None has hot water or generator.

On the hill:

Vista Mar, ✆571.3000. 50 rooms in superior, standard or junior suites; superb views. Well-run hotel with pool, bar, ✗, sunbathing terrace; shuttle to beach until 1800. 5$.

KEY TO STREETS

1 Ayuntamiento
2 Pedro Clisante
3 Duarte
4 Dr Alejo Martínez
5 Dr Rosen
6 David Stern

KEY TO PLACES OF INTEREST

1 Los Almendros
2 Casa del Sol disco
✆ Codetel
✗ P.J.'s Internat. Restaurant
3 Police Station
4 Post Office
5 Sosúa Caribbean Fantasy
6 Sosúa Minigolf
7 Synagogue
✆ Tourist Information
8 Vista Mar

El Mirador, ✆571.2202. 80 rooms in 3 sections; 40 are fully-equipped single or double room villas. All-inclusive resort-complex 10 mins from Sosúa by hotel's free hourly shuttle. Pool, bar, sauna, ✗, disco; evening entertainment. 5$.

Sir Francis Drake Resort, Camino Llibre, ✆571.3010, −3850.

109 rooms, single or double; junior suites with kitchenettes; cable TV, AC; pool, many activities. This hotel opened in March 1988 and is away from the bustle of Sosúa; décor recalls the days of Britain's captain who helped to sink the Spanish Armada. Hourly bus to beach. 5$.

Sosúa Caribbean Fantasy, ✆571.3353, −2534; telex ITT.346.2005.

68 rooms and suites; AC, cable TV. Modern styled hotel at the base of the hill opposite Charamicos; jazzy pool and terrace ✗ Montellano overlooking main road. Short walk to beach; disco in evening. 5$.

In El Batey:

There are many small hotels and guest houses in El Batey, offering an intimate yet independent alternative to the large hotels in other resorts. Most hotels are in quiet sidestreets between private villas, with own pool and restaurant, and minutes from the beach.

There is a **Codetel** office in the village centre, and a good range of restaurants and night spots is within a short walk of the hotels.

Sosúa by the Sea, ✆571.3720; PO Box 361.

71 rooms, including studios, with AC, cable TV, own bathroom; ✗ Sunset Place has sea views. By Playa Chiquita (also known as La Playita, both meaning 'little beach'). 5$

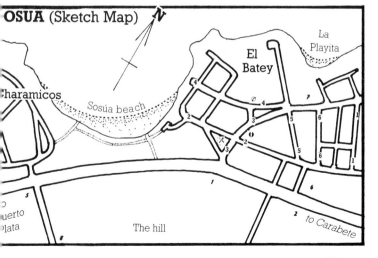

Casa Marina, C/ David Easter, on beachside, ✆571.3131.
66 rooms, but being enlarged. AC, pool, ✖ Los Delfines. 5$.
One Ocean Place, behind the town hall, ✆571.3131.
50 apartments with kitchenettes; AC, cable TV; pool; nice decor; ✖ El Colonial. 5$.
Sea Breeze,, C/ Dr Alejo Martínez, ✆571.3858.
30 rooms, AC, private balconies, kitchenettes; small pool, bar; scooter rental; 24-hour medical service. This mauve-coloured hotel is in town centre. ✖ The Rose Garden has good reputation. 4$.
Sosúa, C/ Dr Alejo Martínez, ✆571.2683.
38 rooms, some with kitchenettes; AC or fan; pool, bar; short walk to beach and town. 4$.
Yaroa, C/ Dr Rosen, ✆571.2651.
24 rooms, AC or fans; good pool, pleasant rooftop area. In quiet street near town centre and beach; good reputation, run by well-established local family. 4$.
Coralillo, C/ Pedro Clisante, Villas Coralillo; ✆ 571.2645, −2625.
42 rooms, 2 suites, plus 4 cabañas with kitchen and 2 bedrooms; AC; pool, terrace restaurant with sea view; night club. 5$.
Playa Chiquita Beach Resort, ✆571.2800.
90 rooms, AC, cable TV; pool with sunken bar; ✖ Hiranya; evening entertainment on terrace. Walking distance from town; on edge of small beach. 4$.
Woody's, C/ Dr Rosen, ✆571.2032.
80 rooms, double or triple; AC; pool with bar. A new property near town centre. 4$.
Los Almendros, on main road; ✆571.3515, −3530.
78 rooms, AC, balcony; pool; ✖ La Casona; many activities; car-rental, large P area. Linked to beach through tunnel. 4$.
Los Charamicos, ✆571.2668, −3969.
91 rooms in two or three-bed apartments or villas; AC, balconies, kitchenettes. 4$.
North Shore, C/ Pedro Clisante, ✆571.2388, −2292.
28 rooms, AC, private bathrooms; pool. Short walk to town centre and beach. 4$.

Apart-hotels:
A selection of the many apart-hotels (efficiencies) in El Batey:
Apart-hotel Alcázar, C/ Dr Rosen 3, ✆571.2512.
12 rooms, fans; pool. Near main road, few minutes' walk to beach. 4$.
Condos Dominicanos Apart-hotel, C/ Ayuntamiento − C/ García; ✆571.2504.
35 rooms, fans, no TV; pool. Near Playa Chiquita. 4$.
Hostal de Lora, C/ Dr Alejo Martínez, ✆571.3939.32 rooms, AC, no TV; pool. Short walk to beach. Breakfast included. 4$.

Guest houses:

A selection of the many small hotels and guest houses:

Koch's Ocean Front Guest House, C/ Alejo Martínez, ✆571.2234.

9 cabañas and 4 rooms. Functional. Well-known house opposite Hotel Sosúa. 4$.

Auberge du Village Inn, C/ Dr Rosen 8, ✆571.2569.

7 rooms, fans; pool in tropical garden. Family style set-up, clean and tastefully decorated; cultured atmosphere. 4$.

Costa Sol Sosúa, C/ Pedro Clisante, Urbanización Villas A. María; ✆571.3553.

14 standard rooms, 7 studios, AC or fan; pool. 4$.

Sun Island Inn, C/ Ayuntamiento 41, ✆571.2558.

10 rooms, fans, private bathroom; daily maid. Informal atmosphere, close to town and beach. 4$.

Tourist Studio S.A. 12 rooms, fans, own bathrooms and kitchenettes; terrace. 4$.

El Neptuno, La Puntilla, ✆571.2664.

18 fully-furnished apartments with sea view; pool; snack bar. In quiet area. 4$.

Villa:

Seahorse Ranch, ✆571.2374.

This is a private community some 20 minutes east of the airport and set along 2km of shoreline near Sosúa. You'll find landscaped gardens and forest, tennis, riding, water sports and a pool. Accommodation is

You can't complain of overcrowded beaches in the east of the country.

obviously in villas with 24-hour security patrol; phone to see if there are vacancies – or any villas for sale. A hotel is planned here for the early 1990s.

Tourist Information Office. For further information on hotels and other accommodation, contact the Tourist Information Office on C/ Duarte (the main street); the staff speaks English. Or by phone contact Servicios Turísticos Dominicano, ✆(809).571.2665.

Restaurants in El Batey (Sosúa):

There is no shortage of eating-houses in El Batey; Calle Pedro Clisante is packed with them, and many of the hotels have their own on the premises. This selection is from the better-known restaurants.

Morva Mai, C/ Pedro Clisante 5, ✆571.2706.

Renowned for its décor, seafood, and relaxed European atmosphere, with occasional live entertainment. Open all day. 4$.

Café Mama Juana; well-known for its rustic décor and seafood specialities. Open from breakfast to 2400. 4$.

United Fruit Company – **La Roca,** ✆571.2216.

This was a banana warehouse before its tasteful conversion to a restaurant (the United Fruit Company) and disco (La Roca). Meals from 1100-2300 daily; music from 2100–0200 nightly – and popular. Pay to eat and listen free.6$.

P.J's International, C/ Pedro Clisante, ✆571.2325.

In the heart of El Batey, this bar-restaurant serves light meals such as hamburgers. Open until 0200. 2$.

Marco Polo, a terrace restaurant with good beach views; known for its food and décor. 6$.

Restaurants in Charamicos. There are a few restaurants in Charamicos near the beach which are popular with tourists; they are relaxed and charge moderate prices.

Nightlife:

Most of the tourist hotels have discos and a few have night clubs; Toya Jackson has appeared at the Sand Castle night club. In town you'll find La Roca Disco and the Casa del Sol, the latter claiming to be 'the solution to nightlife.' El Batey stays open until late, many bars operating until 0200.

Transport:

Buses: Caribe Tours operates from Charamicos; ✆571.2665.

Guaguas: Catch your guagua on the highway.

Motoconchos: In El Batey motoconchos operate from C/ Duarte – C/ Pedro Clisante near P.J's Restaurant; in Charamicos they start from in front of the police station. Fares: anywhere in El Batey, RD$1; between the two villages, RD$2; add RD$3 to each after 2100.

Auto-rental: General Car Rental at Hotel Los Almendros,

₡571.3515. Santini Rent-a-Car (plus motor-bikes and scooters) in El Batey, ₡571.2376. Rates: 80cc bikes RD$60, 125cc bikes RD$110 per day.

Telephones: Codetel has centres in C/ Duarte and C/ Dr Rosen.

Medical assistance: Sosúa Medical Center, beside One Ocean Place, behind Town Hall (Ayuntamiento), ₡571.2305, −3949. 24-hour service.

24-hour pharmacy: Farmacia San Rafael on Carretera Sosúa-Sabaneta, ₡571.2515.

CABARETE

At first glance you might think Cabarete has opted out of the tourist rat-race and is going its own way: with that superb long beach it is the windsurfing capital of the Dominican Republic and it hosted the World Windsurfing Championships in 1987. But look again; there are two large hotel-resorts to the north of the village, with more being built.

There's no denying the village is quieter and cheaper than its neighbour 9 miles (15km) to the east, for the real Cabarete is simply a sprawl of buildings along the roadside, with a strong French Canadian atmosphere. Many of the bars and small guest houses are Canadian-owned − and charge quite reasonable rates. You can't miss the two large windsurfer centres in the middle of the village, and the Café des Artistes acts as an informal information bureau.

Hotels:

Camino del Sol, ₡571.2858, −2930.

A new project designed to include a hotel, a commercial centre, 123 villas, 507 condos, nine tennis courts, a restaurant, four beach clubs, stables and pool − with its own power plant and water system. Built to high specification and pleasing style beside a splendid beach five minutes west of Cabarete, this is a highly recommended resort for seekers of comfort and some seclusion. 5$.

Punta Goleta: ₡583.5131 on Cabarete, 586.3988 on Pto. Pta, 562.2774 on Sto. Dgo.

126 rooms and 2 villas; semi-olympic pool, many activities; 3 ✗ and bars. Built in 1986 on 100 acres (40ha) of property across the road from a beautiful deserted beach, near a lagoon that attracts many birds. Perfect country retreat but no nightlife. 5$.

Hostería del Rey, 10 rooms, fans; ✗, bar; on beach. 2$.

Restaurant:

Chez Marcel, beachside, specialising in seafood; relaxed.

RIO SAN JUAN

Looking for a tropical paradise? You might find it at Río San Juan, 39 miles (63km) east of Sosúa on a gently-curving peninsula. This quiet and orderly little seaside town is set amid coast and country of such beauty that tourists come just to admire the scenery.

At the end of the high street the Laguna Gri-gri is a picturesque spot where you can hire a boat to take you out to sea or to the beach of La Caleta just beyond the estuary; the lagoon is indeed beautiful, but don't believe all you read in the tourist brochures. Gri-gri, by the way, is a tree that grows in this area but don't be too disappointed if you miss it or the mangroves.

The paradise-hunting visitors have created a demand for short-stay hotels, hence these...

Hotels:

Río San Juan, ✆589.2211, −2379. An attractive building with 38 double rooms, disco El Establo, ✗; pool. Squeaky clean with helpful staff, but I notice a shortage of guests. Half-board, 5$.

Santa Clara, C/ Padre Billini 61, ✆589,2286.

Basic but clean; 20 rooms with private bathroom; mains electricity, no hot water; P for motor-bike. Overpriced in 2$ range.

Apart-hotel San Juan, ✆589.2292, −2223. Suitable for longer stays; two or three-room apartments with bathroom, AC, kitchen with fridge. Opposite the lagoon. 4$.

Restaurants:

Try the elegant Robert's Restaurant Pizzeria opposite Río San Juan Hotel for a meal with wine, or just for a drink. 'Robert' is helpful if you can speak Spanish. 6$ but good. Another recommended place is unpretentious Le Bambu closer to the main road; the Frenchwoman who owns it cooks good food at good prices. For formal eating go to the Río San Juan Hotel.

Nightlife:

Nightlife? Try El Establo disco at the Río San Juan Hotel.

CABRERA

Still looking for paradise? You'll be lucky to find anything to outclass the breathtaking beauty of Cabrera's two north-western beaches, nine miles (14km) away.

Playa Grande is pure desert isle fantasy with its blue and green sea, golden sand, and the backdrop of coconut palms amid luxuriant vegetation, with not a building in sight; even the guagua drop-off in the large, shaded car park is hidden. But nothing is perfect: the waves are moderately strong, and weak swimmers should be cautious − and the developers will soon move in to create another tourist complex.

Who has right of way? A truck driver ignores the 'una via' sign at this Puerto Plata junction.

The locals are very persistent in their attempts to sell to you on this beach and can't understand why you don't want a piña colada at 8 a.m.

Playa La Preciosa, the beach around the headland from Playa Grande, is even more wild and beautiful, offset by a rugged stack to the south-east. No developers on the horizon yet, and the local people insist that the sea has a dangerously strong undertow: be careful if swimming here.

Nearer the village of Cabrera is a charming and secluded beach at the base of the headland of Cabo Francés Viejo, where a small cascade provides a natural shower after your swim. Access is easy by guagua, but there is no parking area.

Cabrera village has nothing to offer, but 5 miles (8km) to the east is Playa El Diamante, another beauty spot with a view towards the Samaná Peninsula, but too shallow and muddy for swimming.

A mile further is the village of La Entrada from where a passable mile-long (1.6km) track leads to a two-mile (3km) stretch of golden sand lying between swaying coconut palms and crystal clear waters, with a clean stream, the Arroyo Salado, running across the beach. Be honest — what more could you ask for?

Hotels:

Hotel-Restaurant Julissa, ✆589.7355. On the main road in Cabrera; 16 rooms, AC or fans, hot water; ✕ and disco next door; P. 1$. On edge of town are the Cabañas Yulissa.

Los Farallones (Hostal Catalina). In Canada ✆ (Montreal) 514.334.3479 for reservations.

An elegant, luxury retreat in the hills two miles (3km) west of Cabrera, with splendid scenery and cooling breezes. Own pool, and minibus service to a different beach each day. Opened in 1988 catering for Canadians but if you can get one of the 12 rooms, grab it. Also has villas for rent. Excellent ✗. 4$.

La Palmeral. In Canada ✆ (Montreal) 514.437.8389 for reservations; the owner is Canadian.

Less sophisticated than Los Farallones, this 16-apartment hotel with beds for up to six people per apartment, operates on the same principle. Newer, lower on the hill; pool and minibus. 4$.

Restaurants: In Cabrera village, Virginia's has a good reputation for local dishes.

Transport: Caribe Tours is at Lorenzo Alvarez 33, in front of the park; guaguas pass through village.

NAGUA

Tourism has bypassed Nagua and it's easy to see why. River sediments cloud the waters of the bay, and the town has no beach. West, Playa Boba is rather unkempt and access is down a mile-long track, but five miles (8km) east the golden sands start again. Nagua is therefore likely to remain a typical Dominican town and worth a stop-off for that reason, but don't come especially.

Hotels:

Hotel Doña Viola, just off the bypass; nine rooms; AC or fans but no generator; family-type, run by the doña herself, and the best choice in Nagua. 1$.

There are other 1$ hotels in town, such as Cervantes, Atahualpa, San Carlos, but the locals use them for romantic purposes.

Carib Caban, ✆584.3145. Five miles (8km) east, amid beachside palms; owner is Austrian woman. Squeaky clean, smart décor, quiet; four-poster double beds and private bathrooms; generator but no hot water. Smart ✗. Tariff is per person including two meals, 3$.

Transport: Metro Tours, ✆584.2857, Cafetería Mayra, C/ Colón, facing Banco de Reservas; Caribe Tours, ✆584.2379, facing park in C/ Colón. Guaguas to Samaná, Pto. Pta, S. Fco de Macoris.

SANCHEZ

Sánchez is a beautiful town slumbering away amid memories of when it had a rail link to San Fransisco de Macoris and La Vega. Its huge wooden houses look as if they belong in the southern states of the USA rather than in a sleepy Dominican town that history has left behind. Sánchez is unaffected by tourism: the thousands of visitors to the Samaná Peninsula just go straight by.

Sánchez factfile:
Hotel La Costa, Av Libertad. 10 rooms, AC or fan; generator and cistern; on raised ground so has breeze; interior patio. 1$.
Caribe Tours, Av Libertad 7, facing park; ✆552.7434.
Codetel, C/ Duarte 4.

THE SAMANA PENINSULA
LAS TERRENAS

The tourist industry has just discovered Las Terrenas and is beginning to convert this sleepy Dominican village into a small cosmopolitan town where Europeans – mostly French – run the many hostels and small hotels. The main beach is top grade, sheltered by a reef 100m offshore and running 2½ miles (4km) east to the village of El Portillo, and west to the headland which separates it from the next beach, Playa Bonita; the widest sands and deepest water are in the west, accessible by a track that leads past the hotels and cabañas, and the sands improve the further you go; the track ends at a little river near the promontory from where you can cross the headland on foot to Playa Bonita.

The reef guarantees calm waters for bathing and removes the risk of sharks, so young children can play and swim with minimum supervision.

Access. The road from Sánchez is only 10 miles (17km) long from where it leaves the main road to Samaná, but travel is slow because of the hairpin bends and the breathtaking views that they reveal; the surface is of smooth tarmac in keeping with the tourist growth anticipated at Las Terrenas.

Access to Playa Bonita by car: from the town centre drive up the main street towards the hills and look for the sign leading you onto an unsurfaced but adequate road two miles (3km) long, which wanders through lush countryside.

Playa Bonita. Playa Bonita – 'pretty beach' – is aptly named. The waves lap more freely against the sands, unchecked by any reef; the three offshore islands, *Cayos de las Ballenas,* 'Keys (islets) of the Whales,' look like a school of those mammals heading westwards; and even the hotels are beautiful.

Playa Cosón. Turn right on the beach and you come to a picturesque cove which is a little dirty; turn left (west), and the beach leads you round a gentle headland to show you a spectacular emerald-green bay set against a backdrop of darker green mountains. In my opinion this is the most beautiful bay in the Dominican Republic, even more rewarding because it is totally unspoilt and almost unknown. To reach my little piece of heaven, Playa Cosón,

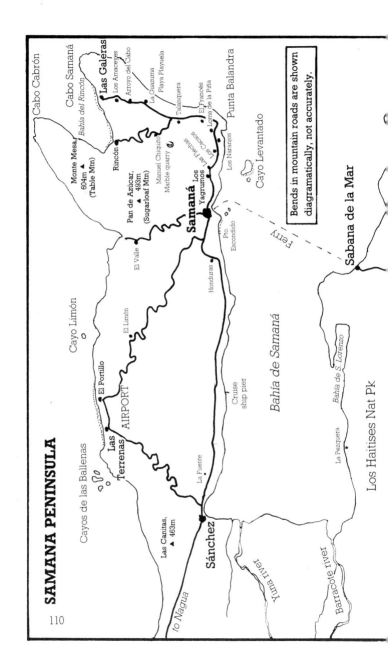

SAMANÁ PENINSULA

110

Cabo Cabrón

Cabo Samaná

Las Galeras

Los Amaceyes
Arroyo del Cabo
La Guazuma
Playa Playuela

Bahía del Rincón

Talanquera

Monte Mesa▲
604m
(Table Mtn)

Rincón

El Francés
Loma de la Piña

Punta Balandra

Pan de Azúcar, 493m
▲ (Sugarloaf Mtn)

Manuel Chiquito
Marble quarry

Las Piedras
Los Cacaos

Los Naranjos

Cayo Levantado

El Valle

Samaná
Los Yagrumos

Pto.
Escondido

Ferry

Sabana de la Mar

| Bends in mountain roads are shown diagramatically, not accurately. |

Cayo Limón

El Portillo

El Limón

AIRPORT

Honduras

Bahía de Samaná

Las Terrenas

Cayos de las Ballenas

La Fuente

Cruise
ship pier

La Pezquera

Bahía de S. Lorenzo

Los Haitises Nat Pk

Las Canitas,
▲ 463m

Sánchez

to Nagua

Yuna river

Barracote river

drive along the sandy track past the Hotel Atlantis.

The entire area around Las Terrenas is utterly charming and is probably the most beautiful spot in the country; it could be the most beautiful in the entire Caribbean! The sand is white, the sea crystal clear, and the vegetation is of jungle-freshness. And to add to that pleasure there are many comfortable hotels, yet you can easily forget you are in a resort at all. This, to me, is a portrait of paradise – don't you dare miss it!

Río Limón Waterfall. The road east from Las Terrenas wanders across country to Samaná, 28 miles (46km) away, passing through the

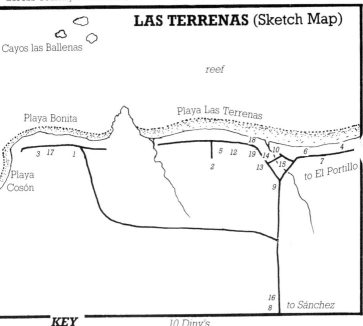

LAS TERRENAS (Sketch Map)

Cayos las Ballenas

reef

Playa Bonita

Playa Las Terrenas

Playa Cosón

to El Portillo

to Sánchez

KEY

1 Acaya Hotel
2 Ananas
3 Atlantis
4 Bar El 28
5 Cacao Beach
6 Casa Blanca
7 Casa Coco
8 Chimichurri stand
9 Comedor Mami
10 Diny's
11 Doña Nina's
12 La Hacienda
13 La Louisiane
14 Modus
15 Nuevo Mundo disco
16 Palacio disco
17 Punta Bonita
18 La Salsa
19 Tropic Bananas

little village of El Limón. Two kilometers past the military post (where you can make enquiries) you'll see children eager to show you the Río Limón waterfall which is at an altitude of around 2,500ft (800m) and which falls about 150ft (50m), splitting into four separate cascades. Allow an hour for this walk — or hire a horse.

Hotels: *In Las Terrenas:*

Las Terrenas and Playa Bonita have a vast range of accommodation on offer from the RD$20-a-night cabaña to the luxury resort of El Portillo which has its own private airport. Las Terrenas also has many private rooms on offer, and a cheap pension or two.

Doña Nina, 8 cabañas with double beds, mosquito nets, home-made gasoline lamps; outdoor shower, water pumped on request; communal latrine. Ideal for young people roughing it and for meeting fellow-travellers. Run by ageing Doña Nina helped by her parrot. On Portillo road east of sea-eroded stretch. 1$.

Hotel Diny, 20 rooms, cooled by sea breeze, in main building above ✗ or in cabañas. On beach at end of village, yet is focal point as most people eat here. Without bathroom, 2$; with, 4$.

Across the little river from Hotel Diny and on sand track along the beach are several hotels, mostly European owned, offering moderate priced cabañas. All are new, small, intimate, tastefully built — and they are in this order:

Louisiane Hotel, clean, nice décor, own separate ✗ Modus Bar-Restaurant, popular with gringos. **Tropic Banana,** reputedly the best in Las Terrenas and with best service. Smart, beach opposite; ✗ (breakfast included); lively bar. 16 cabañas; large P; radio-telephone M-40 #567.5351 (no phones in Las Terrenas). Accepts bookings for charter flights El Portillo — Santo Domingo (3-seater plane costs RD$725). **La Hacienda,** similar to above but not as popular. **Cacao Beach Hotel,** large tourist-resort currently under construction; pool, tennis, ✗. **Ananas,** at end of track; rooms in house or cabañas; pretty but run-down; probably changed hands when you read this.

El Portillo Beach Club, ✆585.0102.

75 rooms in condo or in one- or two-room cabañas with bathroom and kitchen. Luxury, secluded beachside hotel on edge of palm grove; raised pool; ✗ Frutas del Mar; disco, many sports, nightlife. Tariff is all-inclusive, 5$.

This hotel has its own airstrip and air-taxi service to Herrera Airport in Santo Domingo. You may book a flight either way through Prieto Tours which also handles hotel reservations.

In Playa Bonita:

Hotel Acaya, 24 rooms; intimate, looking like large house; beach at front; superb view from open-air bohio bar and ✗. Canadian owner. Cheapest in Playa Bonita; breakfast included; 4$.

112

Punta Bonita Resort, ✆685.0821 Unidad 733, (a *Unidad* number indicates a radio telephone link from Santo Domingo).

9 rooms; two- four- or six-bed; cable TV. Bar downstairs, ✗ upstairs, superb views; squeaky clean. Lawn down to beach; riding, motor-bike rental, minibus. Breakfast included; 4$.

Hotel Atlantis, PO Box 20541, Sto. Dgo. ✆ to Caribelle S.A. 536.6992 for information; radio-phone operates 0900-1900.

11 rooms, in main building or cabañas. Stone-built; resembles country home; bar is pseudo beer-cellar; owners are German and many guests come through Airtours (Germany). 4$.

Restaurants:

There is a wide range of places to eat, from a couple of *comedores* in the main street and a hygienic *chimichurri* stall near the top of town. All restaurants except Diny's are European-run.

Diny's; good food in generous proportions, but menu is limited towards end of day. Open from breakfast with comida criolla. 2$.

Casablanca; good menu with seafood a speciality; smart restaurant in what appears to be a large private beachfront house. 6$.

Casa Coco. French pizzería; tasteful décor, good music, food reasonable. Recommended for the price, 2$.

Bar-Restaurant El 28; good view, good seafood paella served by owner Manuel from Spain. Rustic, bohemian. 4$.

Bar-Restaurant La Salsa; French cuisine from French owners. 6$.

Tropic Banana; fairly extensive menu at good value; popular with European community. 4$.

Nightlife:

Many of the restaurants have bars that stay open late, but there is also the inevitable disco option: El Palacio is small and caters for adolescents; El Nuevo Mundo, on the main road beyond Tropic Banana, is a big open-sided dance floor which attracts Dominicans and tourists alike.

Transport:

Taxis from Sánchez cost RD$80 for three people, camionetas regularly cross the ridge from Séanchez, or for RD$725 you can fly in from Santo Domingo (see El Portillo ✈.) Motor cycles are available at Rent-a-Motor Las Terrenas for the equivalent of US$20, £12, per day. Dominicanada Tours (not a misprint) opposite Casablanca restaurant goes to local spots and big towns.

Codetel: nearest is at C/ Duarte 4, Sánchez.

SAMANA

Foreigners have been coming to Samaná for centuries, but only with the advent of tourism have they been welcome. Christopher

When the going gets tough, the tough stop off for a drink of fresh cool coconut milk.

Columbus — properly, Cristobal Colón — was the first in 1493, his arrival provoking a battle with the native Taino tribe in which the sky was reported as being full of flying arrows. The Spaniards named this secluded inlet *La Bahía de la Flechas,* 'The Bay of Arrows.'

Centuries passed before the Spanish — mostly from the Canary Islands — returned to establish a town on this site in 1756.

Napoleon. French buccaneers had occupied the western third of Hispaniola, and the part now known as Haiti was ceded to them in 1697. The French slaves revolted in 1791 under Toussaint l'Ouverture and drove the Europeans from the island, prompting Napoleon to strike back. Between 1795 and 1804 the emperor planned to capture Samaná, rename it the City of Napoleon and make it the European cultural centre of the Western Hemisphere. The plan failed, and on New Year's Day 1804 Haiti gained its independence, controlling the entire island of Hispaniola.

Slavery. Spain recaptured the eastern two-thirds between 1809 and 1821, then lost it once again to Haiti. As most Haitians are the descendants of black slaves, in their newfound freedom they welcomed slaves escaping from the southern states of the USA, Haiti's President Boyer helping many of them settle in Samaná. The legacy of this American colonisation is that a number of people in the town still speak old American-English.

Ulysses Grant. In 1844 politics split the island for a final time, the eastern part becoming the present Dominican Republic, but foreign intervention had not ceased. By 1870 US President Ulysses Grant wanted to buy the Samaná Peninsula for $1,500,000 from the Dominican president, Buenaventura Báez, and convert it into a naval base; the treaty of annexation was defeated in the US Senate by a mere ten votes.

Samaná was badly damaged by fire in 1946, and further ravaged in the 1970s in an attempt to create what officialdom thought the coming tourist industry would want; thankfully the old Protestant church in the centre of town, built by those freed slaves from America, was spared.

And now in the 1980s the foreigners are back again, investing their money in Samaná and its beautiful peninsula. This time they are welcome, but the town has yet to see the anticipated boom in moneyed visitors; perhaps that will come when the local El Barril airport is extended to take the big jets from faraway places.

The town of Santa Bárbara de Samaná — its full name is seldom-used — is spacious, with a strong European character and, unusual for the Dominican Republic, it is quiet, almost as if the locals have been overwhelmed by the beauty of the place, where mountains covered in coconut palms plunge to beaches of white sand and emerald sea, and every twist in every track offers you another slice of Eden.

Cayo Levantado. Six miles (10km) east and a mile or so offshore is Cayo Levantado, one of three islands, but one that is endowed with a splendid beach; access is by ferry from Samaná's port or from Los Yagrumos beach.

Other beaches. Other beaches of outstanding beauty in the area are Las Galeras, at the end of the tarmac 16 miles (26km) east of Samaná and on the north coast's Bahía El Rincón; El Rincón beach is only a few miles from Las Galeras at the head of the bay, but access is along a seven-mile (12-km) track branching off the tarmac road near Talanquera village. Another outstanding stretch of sand easily reached from Samaná is Puerto Escondido, 'Hidden Port,' tucked in behind the headland on which the Bahía Beach Resort stands.

Roads. The Sánchez — Samaná — Las Galeras road is fine, but the 28 miles (46km) between Samaná and Las Terrenas via El Limón is extremely rough.

Ferry. The passenger and motor-cycle ferry which links Samaná and Sabana de la Mar on the south of Samaná Bay, is popular with people travelling between the peninsula and La Romana; details at the end of the section. Sabana, by the way, has its stress on the middle 'a,' distinguishing it from Samaná, which doesn't.

Whales. If you hire a boat or go on the appropriate excursion from December through to March you're likely to see the overwintering humpback whales in the bay.

A smart motoconcho in Samaná.

Hotels:

Bahía Beach Resort, ✆538.2218, −2424; telex ITT.346.0554.

64 rooms in the main three-storey block plus two suites, six cabañas; pool, ✖ Las Palmeras, disco Puerto Escondido, casino; private beach, excursions to other local beaches for ⚓. On hill overlooking town and port; splendid views over lush vegetation, town and sea; the best maintained of the state-run Corphotels. 4$.

Cotubanama, C/ Fransisco del Rosario Sánchez, ✆538.2558, −2261.

14 simple but adequate rooms; fans. Near basketball pitch by large roundabout at entry to town; family-run. Breakfast included. 2$.

Tropical Lodge, ✆538.2480.

Eight double rooms, AC or fan, private bathroom, some with balconies. Pretty, French-owned hotel just out of town on east extension of the Malecón. Set near coconut grove. Price per room, including breakfast, 4$.

Hotel Kiko, Eight rooms; town centre near Chinese resurant; family-run; generator, fan, private bathroom, no hot water. P. 2$.

Hotel King, C/ Fransisco del Rosario Sánchez, ✆538.2404.

Ten rooms, AC or fan; generator, hot water; by roundabout and set against hillside. Beside ✖ Quioli le Belge. With fan, 2$, with AC 4$.

Hotel Nilka, C/ Santa Bárbara 4, ✆538.2245.

11 rooms; hot water on first floor (US 2nd floor); AC or fan. Beside Codetel office; family-run. 2$.

Private houses. Many people in town rent out rooms in their homes, and some have apartments. For information on these, or on anything else in Samaná, ask one of the young men at the port; for a few pesos these youths act as letting agents and guides. But may I recommend the house of Carmen Kery at Teodoro Chassereaux 6, ✆538.2354; it has 3 double rooms plus use of kitchen, bathroom, living room, and constant electricity and hot water.

Restaurants:

Camilos, El Malecón, ✆538.2495. There is nothing but praise for this restaurant which is squeaky clean down to its restrooms. Open from breakfast time. 2$.

El Chino, C/ Teodoro Chassereaux, off the Malecón, ✆538.2215. This Chinese restaurant has one of the most beautiful views imaginable; good food, generous servings, shrimps are finger-size. Highly recommended. 2$.

Café de Paris, Malecón 6, facing harbour. Pleasant place for Malecón-watching in evening. Ices, light meals; good piazzas but crêpes not recommended. 4$.

Nightlife:

Bars such as the Café de Paris and La Mata Rosada form the mainstay of Samaná's nightlife; the latter is a sophisticated and expensive cocktail bar with piano music from where you can watch strollers on the Malecón. For other music try disco El Cielo or the dance floor called Super Terraza – La Rotonda, beside the Hotel King, noted for its merengue.

La Fuente bar, 15 miles (25km) along the Sánchez road, is worth a visit. The bar is built around a natural spring, a *fuente*, which serves as a swimming-pool.

Transport:

Caribe Tours, El Malecón, ✆538.2229. **Guaguas** leave from the market on Av Fransisco del Rosario Sánchez. **Motoconchos** are in town; look for the Honda 50cc motoconcho attached to a three-wheel canopied carriage seating six.

Ferry. The ferry leaves Samaná at 0730, 1100 and 1500; it leaves Sabana de la Mar at 0930, 1200 and 1700 but, this being the Dominican Republic, these times may not be observed strictly. The crossing takes 60 to 90 minutes and is cancelled in stong winds. Fare is RD$5 per person and RD$10 for a motor-cycle; cars are not carried.

From Samaná port you can take a boat to Cayo Levantado for RD$5; boats are also available for whale-watching or to go across to Haitises National Park. Boats also operate from Yagrumos beach, 4½ miles (7km) east of Samaná to Cayo Levantado or for private hire, but this is economical only for groups.

Festivals:

The *Fiestas Patronales* are on 4 December; the *Fiesta de San Rafael* is on 24 October. The region has several folklore dances and relevant costumes; watch out for El Bambulá, El Chivo Florete and El Oli-Oli.

❶: the state-run **Tourism Information Office** is just off the Malecón behind the Camilo Restaurant, ✆538.2350, −2219. The **Samaná Tourist Service** is at Av La Marina 5, off the Malecón near the Mata Rosada. It's a private enterprise, run by Jean-Pierre Deleuse, and is the place to come to buy a place in a group trip in any of the boats, to go horse-riding, to visit Playa Rincón, or to do anything else for which M. Deleuse can supply a reservation.

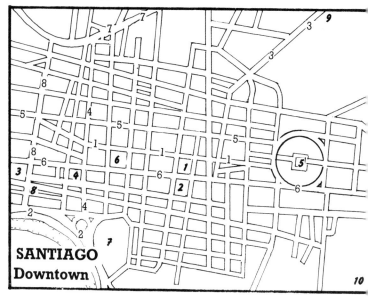

**SANTIAGO
Downtown**

KEY TO STREETS

1 C/ Beller
2 Av Cicunvalación
3 Av Duarte
4 C/ Duarte
5 Av Restauración
6 C/ del Sol
7 Av 27 de Febrero
8 Av 30 de Marzo

KEY TO PLACES OF INTEREST

1 Cathedral of Holy Apostle
2 Columbus Park
3 Duarte Park
4 Market
5 Monument to Heroes of Restoration
6 Post Office
7 San Luis Fort
8 Tobacco Museum
9 Town Hall (Palace)
10 University

14: THE CIBAO VALLEY and the CENTRAL HIGHLANDS

Old-world charm

THE CIBAO is the large fertile valley stretching from La Vega, near the centre of the country, to Monte Cristi in the north-west; it was carved by the Yaque del Norte river, the largest in the Dominican Republic, and it contains the country's second-largest city, Santiago.

SANTIAGO

Founded in 1495 by Bartholomew (Bartolomé) Columbus, elder brother of the explorer, the city of Santiago de los Caballeros — Saint James of the Cavaliers — was destroyed in the earthquake of 1562 and was rebuilt on its present site.

Santiago is a pleasant and relatively affluent city earning its living from the products of the Cibao; the valley yields sugar cane and tobacco which Santiago converts into rum, cigarettes and cigars. The city is home to the *Universidad Católica Madre y Maestra,* reputed to be among the best in the country, and it now has a successful industrial Free Zone.

The city elders have not made the mistake of confusing progress with the destruction of history, so modern Santiago retains a wide range of architectural styles with particular emphasis on the wooden neo-classical turn-of-the-century houses that could have been torn down to make way for concrete and glass. Elegance remains, too, in the larger hacienda-style homes, in the cathedral with its carved mahogany altar, and in the horse-drawn carriages which still roll along the streets.

El Monumento. A notable landmark is the monument to the heroes of the restoration, bearing murals by Vela Zanetti and dominating the entire town. The monument commemorates the War of Restoration of 1865 when the country freed itself from a brief period of Spanish annexation.

Museums. There are museums, too: the *Museo de Arte Folklórico*

Tomas Morel, the Museum of Traditional Art, displaying a collection of carnival masks and other treasures in a beautiful old house near the town centre. The *Museo del Tabaco,* the Tobacco Museum, just beyond the Duarte Park at the corner of 30 de Marzo and 16 de Agosto streets, gives the full story of tobacco from field to factory; many of the world's knowledgeable cigar smokers now claim that Santiago's cigars are as good as those from Cuba. The *Museo de la Villa de Santiago,* the City Museum, records the history of the town and is suitably located in the 19th-cent Palacio Consistoriál, a museum-piece in its own right. And finally there is a downtown cultural centre and, on the banks of the Yaque, the old fort of San Luís.

The tempo of the city is leisurely, and the spirit of the people reflects the belief that life is here to be enjoyed. In the evenings the locals stroll the Calle El Sol, the main street runnning from El Monumento down to Parque Duarte, and at weekends those who can afford not to work escape to Puerto Plata or to the cool alpine beauty of the mountains at Jarabacoa.

Tourism has not affected Santiago to any noticeable degree, and the city is one of the few in the country able to thrive without the direct invasion of tourists, with the result that foreigners here are treated as equals and can blend with the crowds: there are no *limpiabotas* − shoe-shine boys − or self-appointed guides to bother you. That sort of behaviour is not tolerated in this proud city.

HOTELS:

Hotel Camino Real, C/ El Sol, ✆583.4361; Telex ITT.346.0529.

72 rooms, including 9 suites, AC; ✗ El Hidalgo with panoramic city view; piano bar Las Nubes. A tall, modern building in the middle of the main street; much used by businessmen. 4$.

Hotel Don Diego, Av Estrella Sahdala, ✆582.7186.

36 rooms with AC and TV; pool, tennis, disco, ✗ Chinese-creole. A characterless building on the road to Puerto Plata. 3$.

Hotel Matum, by El Monumento, ✆582.3107, Telex ITT.346.1037.

52 rooms, AC, cable TV; pool, disco La Nuit, casino, Spanish patio; also stages shows. Considered the most comprehensive hotel in Santiago with good location; old-style Dominican building a little the worse for wear. 4$.

Hotel Mercedes, C/ 30 de Marzo, ✆583.1171−2.

40 rooms, single, double, triple, AC or fan; water and electricity can be temperamental. Beautiful old wooden building with stained glass and elegant domed entrance hall; town centre site. P at rear. 3$.

Restaurants:

Pez Dorado, C/ El Sol 43, ✆582.2518.

Santiago has some of the most elegant restaurants in the country and many locals claim this one gives the best value. Chinese and

120

seafood. 4$.

Restaurant Osteria, Av 27 de Febrero, ✆582.4165. Probably the most exclusive in town; Italian cuisine. 6$.

El Hidalgo, C/ El Sol, ✆583.4361. International cuisine; elegant. 4$.

L'Elysée, near Columbus Park on C/ del Sol. Attractive French restaurant in a fine old house. 4$.

For cheaper places to eat try the terrace restaurants near El Monumento, or go to a comedor in the city centre.

Nightlife:
Many young people go to the bars and terrace restaurants around El Monumento and then move on to nightspots such as Discoteca Jet Set at Autopista Duarte 2km, or Discoteca La Antorcha at C/ 27 de Febrero 58. The Duarte highway entry to town is home to several nightclubs and discotheques.

Transport:
Caribe Tours, Av Estrella Sadhalá – C/ #10, ✆583.9197–8. Metro Tours, Av Juan Pablo Duarte – Av Maimón, ✆583.4611, 587.4711.

Festivals:
Santiago is famous for its carnivals because the people dress in local costumes known as *lechones,* respresenting mischievous devils; the lechones are brightly-coloured with masks carrying a pair of horns. Carnivals are around 27 February and 16 August, the latter being the *Aniversario de la Restauración,* recalling the country's escape in 1865 from Spanish annexation. The *Fiestas Patronales* (festival of the patron saint), *Santiago Apostol,* St John the Apostle, are on 25 July.

Telephones: Codetel offices at Av Estrella Sadhalá and Av Circunvalación 21.

THE CIBAO
The Cibao stretches down to the sea at Monte Cristi, taking in the valley of the Río Yaque del Norte, but it also includes the headwaters of other streams, notably the Río Yuna which flows east into the Bay of Samaná. For the most part it is a fertile and well-watered region yielding much of the country's farm produce and supporting the moderately-wealthy towns of **Moca, Salcedo, San Fransisco de Macoris** and **La Vega,** the latter lying south-east of Santiago on the upper reaches of the Yuna river.

For a splendid view of the Cibao valley, climb the Santo Cerro, a hill with the church of the same name at its summit and standing 3 miles (5km) north of La Vega.

Hotels. All the towns in the Cibao are untouched by tourism and so reflect the true Dominican atmosphere, and all have acceptable hotels. In La Vega, try the Hotel San Pedro or the Hotel Astral, cheap and clean family-run establishments centrally located on the quiet street of Nuñez de Cáceres. For meals you cannot beat the down-to-earth Comedor Rey at the end of C/ Independencia.

To the west of Santiago are the rural towns of **Esperanza, Mao** and **Sanabeta,** all linked by excellent roads. Mao has the state-run Hotel Cahoba, ✆572.3357, and Sanabeta, also known as Santiago Rodriguez, has the Hotel Marien, ✆580.2489.

CENTRAL HIGHLANDS

The Central Highlands — the Cordillera Central — is a world of mountain streams, of waterfalls set amid cool pine forests, and of rugged mountain peaks, making it almost impossible to believe that this is the tropics and not part of some higher-latitude mountain wilderness such as the Swiss Alps or the Appalachians. Wealthy Dominicans have built their weekend retreats in the mountains, particularly around Jarabacoa, and have added to the alpine effect by choosing Swiss-chalet architecture.

Pico Duarte. Pico Duarte, at 10,417ft (3,177m) the Caribbean's highest peak, dominates the region, throwing a challenge to all adventurers willing to make the three-day hike necessary to reach its summit. If this is for you, go to the village of La Ciénega to hire your guide. Three other impressive peaks, all above 10,000ft (3,000m), pierce the clouds in the Duarte massif.

Jarabacoa. Spring seems to linger all year round in Jarabacoa, a town that has a rugged Wild West feel to it yet is becoming sophisticated with the influx of visitors along the new highway from Las Vegas. The town is a perfect base for a holiday on foot or horseback.

Hotels. The **Pinar Dorado,** ✆Jarabacoa 547.2820 or Sto.Dgo. 689.5105, is an attractive modern building of 85 reasonably-comfortable rooms on the Constanza road; pool in the garden, P, cafeteria-restaurant; 4$. Nearby is the Salto de Jimenoa, a waterfall in which you can bathe.

Hotel Montaña, a state run Corpshotel on La Vega road; run-down and usually nearly empty, but marvellous views. 2$.

Alpes Dominicanos, 132 rooms, new; in pine forest between La Vega and Jarabacoa at 1,500ft (500m); villas or apartments. 3$.

The Placencia at C/ Libertad 32 is one of several restaurants, and there is no shortage of discos. Head for the square and look around: it's a small town so you won't get lost.

Constanza. Set in a high, wide valley, Constanza is an ordinary town with a down-to-earth appearance, where tractors trundle down the main road and the smell of garlic hangs in the air. The people grow potatoes, apples, strawberries, vegetables and flowers but, surprisingly, Constanza has a noisy discothèque, two good restaurants and several hotels. Visitors spend their time walking in the stunningly-beautiful countryside and visiting the Aguas Blancas waterfall 12 miles (20km) away: if you want to join them, head out on the San José de Ocoa road past the Nueva Suiza Hotel and at the road junction fork left; the right fork leads to a ford.

Hotels. The **Nueva Suiza Hotel**, ✆539.2233, stands in grandiose silence and isolation 2km out of town (see above); large state run affair, empty and in need of restoration; 59 rooms, terrace, private bathroom, splendid views. 2$. The ideal retreat for a novelist?

In town are Mi Cabaña above the restaurant and disco at the end of the main street: the ✗ is good but the hotel calls for ear plugs.

There's another ✗ in the street behind, passing the military garrison; sandwiches here are excellent.

Ignoring the disco, curiosity may induce you to explore what appears to be a witch's cottage in a field off the San José de Ocoa road; it's a Wild West style bar.

Roads. The road between La Vega and Jarabacoa is perfect; to Constanza is reasonable but not asphalted – and the views are superb. Alternatively, leave the Autopista Duarte after Bonao and go via El Río; the road is tough with steep climbs, but the view of the reservoir at Hatillo yields dividends.

A marlin adorns the clean, airy lobby of the Luperón Beach Resort Hotel.

Christopher Columbus surveys the Columbus Park in Santo Domingo. He called Hispaniola 'the most beautiful land that human eyes have ever seen.'

15: SANTO DOMINGO and BOCA CHICA

The sleeper awakes

TWENTY YEARS AGO Santo Domingo was a small, sleepy city, forgotten by the rest of the world. Culturally dull, economically backward, and still recovering from the excesses of its dictator-general, Rafael Trujillo, Santo Domingo was on nobody's itinerary.

Today, all that has changed. The capital of the Dominican Republic is now the largest city in the Caribbean with an ever-growing population fast approaching the two million mark. 'La Capital,' as the Dominicans call it, has seen an economic boom part fuelled by foreign money brought in by tourism, and the recent surge in population is now sending the city's boundaries deep into the farmland to the west, north and east.

Pollution. Sadly, some of the newer developments are of poor quality, with slums erupting on the unused land along the banks of the Río Ozama; the almost uncontrollable growth has also put intense strain on all the city's facilities so that power failures, water shortages and atmospheric pollution from traffic are now part of everyday life.

Transport. The independent tourist's first impression of La Capital is of chaos, mainly caused by the near total lack of an adequate public transport system. There is no railway, no tramway, no metro — not even a bus network. The ordinary citizen's option is to jostle for a place on a crowded *carro público,* while the more affluent tourist has the choice of joining the fray or taking a taxi. The result? Frustration for the locals, while the visitor will find a day in the city exciting but very tiring; it's advisable to book in early at a peaceful hotel to recuperate at the end of the day.

First city. Santo Domingo was the first city of the New World, founded by Bartholomew Columbus, Christopher's elder brother, in 1496 as Nueva Isabela, recalling the destruction of that original Villa Isabela on the north coast. And at the approach of the 500th anniversary of Columbus's landing on Hispaniola, in 1492, the Dominican Government has been restoring the oldest parts of the city and improving the remainder of the capital in an attempt to make it worthy of its place in history. The first city in the USA was St Augustine, Florida, founded in 1515.

Nueva Isabela. The early settlers on this island of Hispaniola migrated from the north coast to the Haina river, 12 miles (20km) west of the present Santo Domingo, in their never-ending search for gold. They found a convenient site for a settlement on the east bank of the Ozama river and began building their 'New Isabela,' named from the Spanish queen: the large flour mill of Molinos Dominicanos now occupies the site.

Isabela la Católica. In 1502 the settlers moved to the west bank; while the reason is not recorded we may guess the original town was destroyed by a hurricane, or the newer site was easier to defend. Governor Nicolás de Ovando began this *new* new city, using stone to build ramparts, a fortress, houses, and a home for this outpost of government in Their Catholic Majesties' empire. Some of the buildings remain, and are in the streets called the *Calle de las Damas* and *Isabela la Católica.*

Golden years. For the next 30 years Santo Domingo was the administrative centre of the Spanish Crown in the New World. It was from here that further voyages of discovery were planned and executed, taking Spain's rule around the Caribbean and into Central and South America — and to Florida. These were the golden years, when Santo Domingo reigned unrivalled and was the automatic site of Spain's first institutions in the New World, including the first university, cathedral, mint and hospital.

Sir Francis Drake. But as new lands were discovered and vast treasures in gold were found in Mexico and Peru, Santo Domingo went into decline as its own gold production was tiny. Mexico City became the new centre of administration, power and wealth for the Spaniards, and the final *coup de grâce* awaited Santo Domingo: the arrival in 1586 of the English sailor-explorer Sir Francis Drake, who destroyed much of the city and held the remainder to ransom. From then on, Santo Domingo and Hispaniola survived mainly from the export of wood, sugar and other agricultural products. Spain ignored the city, and it gradually fell into obscurity.

Treaty of Ryswick. While French pirates gradually took control of the abandoned western third of Hispaniola, France was doing badly in Europe, and on 20 September 1697, French diplomats were forced to meet their English and Spanish counterparts at Ryswick, near The Hague (Netherlands), and sign the Treaty of Ryswick. It was a humiliation for French interests in Europe but it gave them the territory of 'Saint Domingue,' now known as Haiti.

Toussaint L'Ouverture. The French cultivated Saint Domingue intensively, importing thousands of African slaves to work in the sugar plantations, but the French Revolution so weakened their hold on their overseas possessions that in 1791 the slave François Dominique Toussaint, 'Toussaint L'Ouverture' (he got his last name from the opening, *ouverture,* he made in the enemy lines) led a revolt which drove the French Royalists and the Spanish from Hispaniola. Toussaint abolished slavery and was working for peace and prosperity, but this praiseworthy effort in social progress brought the island into economic decay as there was nobody to do the heavy work. Toussaint? The French, who briefly returned, captured him in 1802 and he died in a dungeon in the Jura the following year.

Juan Pablo Duarte. Haiti regained its independence in 1804, with Spain once again ruling the eastern part of the island from Santo Domingo, but Haiti gradually extended its influence until yet again it ruled all of Hispaniola. Then in 1844 Juan Pablo Duarte led the struggle which resulted in Dominican independence. Duarte, with his associates Fransisco del Rosario Sánchez and General Matias Ramón Mella, formed the first constitutional republic and are considered as the country's founding fathers; their tombs are in Independence Park in the heart of the city and their names are seen in streets, roads and villages throughout the land.

Dictators. But the future was troubled. The Dominican Republic was plagued by a series of dictators and corrupt governments that led the country into financial ruin; this was the era of people such as Pedro Santana, Buenaventura Báez and Ulises Heureaux. Impoverishment led to occupation in 1861 when Spain annexed the country, holding on to it until the War of Restoration of 1865.

American occupation. The next occupation began in 1916 when the United States took control to regularise the country's finances and collect some overdue debts. The Americans, who stayed until 1924, bequeathed the Dominican Republic a much-improved transport and communications infrastructure.

Rafael Trujillo. And then came Rafael Leonidas Trujillo Molina who seized power in 1930, the year in which Santo Domingo was severely damaged by a hurricane. The need to make the city rise again, combined with Trujillo's passion for building, explains much of the 1930s architecture evident today.

Ciudad Trujillo. Trujillo was a savage dictator, but also a shrewd and hardworking leader who managed to pay off the country's foreign debt. Yet his attitude to wealth was feudal in that what belonged to the country belonged to him; it was said that he became the owner of one huge *finca* (farm) — the Dominican Republic itself — and in 1937 he changed the name of the capital city to Ciudad Trujillo. The obelisk which looks like a miniature version of the one in Washington, D.C, was built on the Malecón to commemorate this megalomaniac's vanity.

Yet during the Trujillo era the city of Santo Domingo prospered and grew, and in 1955 the dictator organised a World Fair in his capital. But on 30 May, 1961, Trujillo was assassinated and the country quickly fell into political instability eventually leading to the 1965 civil war, which was fought mostly on the capital's streets.

U.S. Marines. For the second time in the country's history the USA intervened, sending in the Marines, but only for a short while until political stability was restored.

Expansion. Since the mid-sixties the Dominican Republic has had relatively stable democratic government, and has expanded in wealth and in population. Museums, and the Teatro Nacional, were built; in the mid-seventies came the International Airport of Las Américas, and more recently the country has vastly expanded its tourist industry, with the number of hotel beds continuing to increase year by year; the Dominican Republic will be ready to meet the anticipated flood of visitors for the coming 500th anniversaries, in 1992 of Christopher Columbus's arrival, and in 1996 Bartholomew Columbus's founding of what is now Santo Domingo.

SANTO DOMINGO TODAY

The modern city is divided into two main parts, ignoring its spreading suburbs; the small Zona Colonial which is in essence the Nueva Isabela of Columbus's era, and the 20th-cent expansion. Each is distinct, yet each has its attractions for the visitor.

THE COLONIAL ZONE

The heart of the Colonial Zone is Calle El Conde, running roughly east-west across the old city. A narrow street, now pedestrianised, it is lined with some of the best shops in the capital, interspersed with bars. Near its eastern end is the **Parque de Colón,** Columbus Park (it really means Columbus Square), holding the **Catedral Primada de América,** the 'First Cathedral of America' also known as the Cathedral of Santa María la Menor, completed in 1540 and reputedly holding the remains of Christopher Columbus in a decorative sarcophagus built in 1898.

If the cathedral were to be transported overnight to Spain, it would be no more impressive than the average parish church; it has none of the grandeur of El Pilar in Zaragoza or the cathedral in Mexico City.

Work began in 1523 under Bishop Alexandro Geraldini, and in the short seven years of its building it managed to incorporate Gothic vaults, Romanesque arches and a façade that is pure Renaissance; tradition claims that Bishop Rodrigo de Bastidas laid the final stone over the north door. Although it has 14 chapels it never was a great building either in size or in architecture.

Its importance is due solely to its position as the New World's oldest cathedral; in 1542 Pope Paul III decreed it to be the 'First Cathedral of the Indies' with an authority that surmounted all others in the hemisphere; Pope Benedict XV was later to raise it to the status of basilica.

Sir Francis Drake had little respect for this outpost of Catholicism and during his brief control of the city, with the cathedral as his headquarters and St Peter's Chapel as his jail, he smashed the nose and hand off the statue of Bishop Bastidas.

The Cathedral today. There are no crowds of modern travellers admiring the building; you can wander in at almost any time to see the First Cathedral's treasures which range from Bishop Bastidas's mahogany throne, claimed to be the work of Amerind craftsmen, to a large and varied collection of works of art. The collection's main exhibit is a processional tabernacle which was first carried through the city's streets on Corpus Christi, 1542, with later displays including woodcarvings, oil paintings, gold and silver ware, and jewellery.

The Columbus controversy. The main attraction in the cathedral is undoubtedly the marble and bronze monument and sarcophagus which holds the mortal remains of Christopher Columbus, the man who found America and thought it was China.

Or does it?

Columbus died in Valladolid, Spain, on 20 May 1506, and was buried in the Carthusian Monastery of Sana María de las Cuevas in Seville. Years passed until María de Toledo, Christopher's widowed daughter-in-law, brought the remains back to Santo Domingo, arriving on 9 September 1544. María reinterred the remains in the cathedral beside those of her husband Diego Columbus, the Viceroy of Spain who had died in 1526.

When the Treaty of Basle ceded Santo Domingo to France, the Spanish overlords exhumed Christopher's remains and took them to Havana, Cuba, for reburial in colonial Spanish soil in January of 1796; legend claims that they stayed there until 1898, four years before Cuban independence, when they were taken on their last journey back to Seville.

Padre Fransisco Billini. On 10 September 1877, Padre Fransisco Billini was supervising some maintenance work on the floor of the First Cathedral of the Americas when one of the workers found a small crypt, only a handspan from the spot where Columbus's bones had lain until 1796. This crypt held an urn, and in the urn were the ashes of Christopher Columbus; at least, the Bishop of Santo Domingo, Haiti and Venezuela declared them so and recorded Padre Billini's discovery for posterity. The official Dominican line, then, is that the ashes of Christopher Columbus lie in this marble sarcophagus in the First Cathedral of the New World in Santo Domingo. It might be wrong – but it's such a good story it *ought* to be true. And Padre Billini? He is remembered in street names across the land.

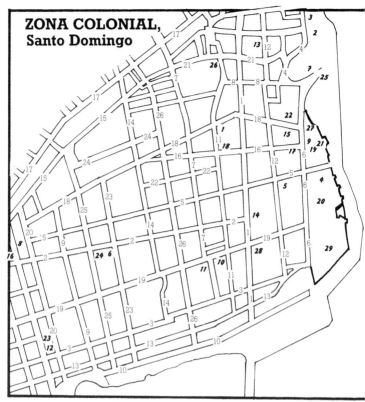

ZONA COLONIAL, Santo Domingo

KEY TO STREETS

1 C/ Arzobispo Meriño
2 C/ Arzobispo Nouel
3 C/ Arzobispo Portes
4 C/ La Atarazana
5 C/ El Conde
6 C/ Las Damas
7 C/ Duarte
8 C/ Emiliano Tejera
9 C/ Espaillat
10 Av George Washington
11 C/ Hostos
12 C/ Isabel la Católica

13 C/ José García
14 C/ José Reyes
15 C/ Juan Perez
16 C/ Gral Luperón
17 Av Mella
18 C/ Las Mercedes
19 C/ Padre Billini
20 C/ Palo Hincado
21 C/ Restauración
22 C/ Salome Ureña
23 C/ Sánchez
24 C/ Santiago Rodriguez
25 C/ Santome
26 C/ 19 de Marzo

KEY TO PLACES OF INTEREST

1 Altagracia Church
2 Ataranza Gate
3 Ataranza Monument
4 Bastidas House
5 Borgella Palace
6 Carmelite Church
7 Columbus's Monument
8 Conde Gate
9 Dávila House
10 Dominican Friars' Convent
11 Dominican Order, 3rd, Chapel of
12 Door of Mercy
13 Duarte Museum
14 First Cathedral of the Americas
15 Gargoyles House
16 Independence Park
17 National Mausoleum
18 Nicolás de Barí Hospital (ruins)
19 Ovando House
20 Ozama Fortress
21 Remedios Chapel
22 Royal Houses Museum
23 Sabana Tower
24 San André's Church
25 San Diego Gate
26 San Fransisco Monastery
27 Sundial
28 Tostado House & Museum of Dominican Family
29 Tower of Homage

El Conde. El Conde's western end is at the **Puerta del Conde,** the original gate in the old city walls and the entry to the newer town. Beyond it lies the modern **Parque Independencia,** in the centre of which are the tombs of Duarte, Sánchez and Mella with a permanent guard of honour.

At its eastern end, El Conde crosses **Calle las Damas,** an ancient cobbled street full of old-world charm; vehicles are not allowed in, giving peace by day and an eery solitude by night. The street gives access to the large **Fortaleza Ozama,** the Ozama Fortress, the oldest stone fort in the New World, built by Ovando to defend his tiny settlement. Open daily until 1700, its courtyard is impressively large for its time.

Within the fortress, the **Torre del Homenaje,** the 'Tower of Homage,' retains its two-metre-thick walls, and some of the cannon that were mounted in the embrasures facing the Ozama river. Despite its weaponry, the tower was actually used for signalling homage — subservience — to visiting ships.

Beside the tower stands the **Casa de Bastidas,** the home of one of the great *conquistadores,* still with its beautiful interior courtyard. The house now holds Planarte, a handicraft centre which has many items on sale.

Further north along Calle las Damas are two beautiful old *casas,* one converted to the **Hostal Nicolás de Ovando** (see 'Hotels,' following) while the other, **La Casa de Francia** where Hernando Cortés, the conqueror of Mexico, is supposed to have planned his campaigns, is now a cultural institute.

Opposite the hostal is the **Panteón Nacional,** the 'National Mausoleum,' which began life in 1748 as a Jesuit Church and has had several roles since, including a tobacco warehouse and a theatre.

On the corner with Calle las Mercedes is **El Museo de las Casas Reales,** the 'Museum of the Royal Houses,' which opened in 1976 holding exhibits of weapons, armour, and maps from three centuries of colonial life, around the main attraction, a cornucopia of treasures salvaged from galleons sunk along the Dominican coasts. Among those wrecks which have yielded their cargoes are the *Guadeloupe* and the *Conde de Tolosa,* both lost in 1724, and the *Concepción* which sank in 1641.

The sundial opposite the museum was built in 1753 and placed so that it was visible to judges in session in the Royal Audience and Court of Appeal which was formerly held here.

Palacio de los Capitanes. The museum is still known by an earlier name, the Palacio de los Capitanes, recalling that in colonial days it served successively as the palace of governors and captains-general, the Royal Audience, the Court of Appeal, the Royal Counting House and the Treasury.

At the northern end of Calle las Damas, to the left of the Puerta (Gate) de San Diego which opens onto the river, is the impressive **Alcázar de Colón,** 'Columbus's Royal Residence,' built between 1509 and 1512. It was named not for the famous father but for his eldest son Diego who, with his vice-reine María de Toledo, was Governor and Viceroy of the West Indies. The Alcázar, its 22 rooms decorated with valuable tapestries and period furniture, has had a superb restoration and is now open to the public until 1700hrs, with guides speaking several languages.

Behind the Alcázar is **Calle La Atarazana,** originally the site of royal arsenals and warehouses, and customs houses. Its colonial buildings now serve as art galleries, gift shops, restaurants and bars.

West, where Calle Emiliano Tejera crosses Calle Isabel la Católica, the Banco Popular now occupies the **Casa del Cordón,** the oldest European-built stone house in Santo Domingo and perhaps in the New

World, dating from 1503. Its name comes from the cord of the Fransiscan Order, which is carved above the door, and it was here that the wealthy ladies of Nueva Isabela gave their jewellery to Drake as ransom for the city.

The ruins of the **Monasterio de San Fransisco,** the first monastery to be built in the Americas, stand at the western end of Calle Emiliano Tejera; here the Indian leader Enriquillo was educated by the Fransiscan friars but in 1881 the building became an institution for the insane, and the remains of cells and their gruesome chains are still visible. Calle Hostos leads south to the ruins of the **Hospital Nicolás de Barí,** founded in 1503.

Enriquillo. In an era when most problems were solved by the sword, Enriquillo was a man of peace. He and his wife Mencia were slaves to a Spanish dignitary, but when the Spaniard's son tried to rape Mencia, Enriquillo escaped with her to the mountains and gathered a party of fellow-fugitives.

The Spaniards sent troops to kill him, but each time Enriquillo captured the Europeans, disarmed them, and sent them back unharmed. Eventually Carlos I of Spain heard of this remarkable 'savage' and sent his envoy, Fransisco de Barrionuevo, to offer the Indian a knighthood and lands for his own peoples. Barrionuevo eventually found his man on the island of Cabrito in what is now Lake Enriquillo, and the Indian chose to accept territory in the Sierra de Baoruco, which he ruled as Don Enriquillo until his death in 1533.

Anacaona. Enriquillo was not unique in his peaceful approach to the warlike European colonists, but the story of Anacaona is one that ended in tragedy. Nicolás de Ovando, Governor of Hispaniola from 1502, was so convinced the Amerinds were planning an uprising that he decided to murder their leaders. Princess Anacaona, reputed to be the most beautiful woman on the island, greeted Ovando's troops with song and dance, but she was hanged without mercy. The only disagreement is where she died – in the mountains around Jaragua, or at a public execution in what is now Duarte Park in the Colonial City and, incidentally, the spot where Sir Francis Drake hanged two Dominican friars.

Convento de los Dominicos. Back in the Zona Colonial, Calle Padre Billini parallels Calle El Conde to the south. Where it crosses Calle Hostos you will find the Convento de los Dominicos, the 'Convent of the Dominican Friars,' completed in 1532 and later the seat of the first university in the New World; the accompanying church is considered to be the oldest in the Western Hemisphere and the altar-piece, a gift from Carlos V of Spain, who was also Holy Roman Emperor, bears the Hapsburg eagle. The astrological symbols on the ceiling of the rosary chapel have baffled historians.

On the eastern border of Duarte Park, the possible site of

'La Catedral Primada,' the First Cathedral of the New World, slumbers in Columbus Park in Santo Domingo.

Anacaona's execution, stands the **Casa de Tostado,** on the corner with Calle Arzobispo Meriño. This colonial house belonged to a prominent family of the time and was among the most beautiful in the old city. The later occupants are remembered in the casa's present function as the Museum of the 19th Century Dominican Family, holding an impressive display of wickerwork and mahogany furniture of the Victorian era: while Victoria was never queen of the Dominican Republic, many of her Jamaican subjects migrated to Santo Domingo bringing their ideas of Victorian living.

The *original* family who lived here saw a son killed by Drake and a daughter's lover murdered in the well in the enclosed garden; it's become traditional to make a wish for good fortune in love as you stand by this well.

The Borgella Palace. The largest monument to the Haitian occupation of the Dominican Republic stands on Calle Isabella la Católica at a right-angle to the cathedral and facing the Parque Colón. This, the Palacio de Borgella, was built during the 1822-44 regime as the occupying power's headquarters, and it remained the seat of government of an independent Dominican Republic until the completion of the Palacio Nacional in 1947. It now holds the National School of Fine Arts.

Verdict. American visitors find the Colonial Zone a fascinating insight into five centuries of history, while European visitors, whose daily lives are spent amid relics going back two thousand years or more, find old Santo Domingo lacking much architectural splendour, but all visitors whose sense of imagination can be stirred appreciate the associations of the past. Columbus, Ponce de Léon, Balboa, Pizarro, Drake, and many more characters from history, walked these streets and lived in these houses, a fact which places Santo Domingo with Havana and Mexico City among the leading communities in the conquest of the Americas. Sadly for the Colonial Zone, those other two cities have much more history to offer.

THE MODERN CITY

Av George Washington begins on the southern edge of the Colonial City and runs west along the shoreline – Santo Domingo has no beach – until, in the middle of the new city, it becomes the Autopista 30 de Mayo. Av George Washington is a prestigious, wide, palm-lined boulevard better known to Dominicans as El Malecón, the prom-enade. It is home to many restaurants, nightclubs and luxury hotels, and is the pulsing jugular vein of this rapidly expanding city.

The Malecón never sleeps, and is at its most explosively exhuber-ant during *Carnaval* and the Merengue Festival, but at any time a stroll along this intriguing, captivating highway is an experience of the very essence of Santo Domingo.

Plaza de Cultura. North of El Malecón along Av Máximo Gómez, and bordered by Av César Nicolás Penson on the south and by Av Dr Pedro Henríquez Ureña on the north, is the Plaza de Cultura, originally the site of Trujillo's mansion but now home to the *Museo Nacional de la Historia Natural*, the *Museo Nacional de Historia y Geografia*, and the *Museo del Hombre Dominicano*, the last one translating as the Museum of Dominican Man; there's also the *Bibliotéca Nacional*, (National Library); the *Galeria de Arte Moderno*, (Gallery of Modern Art) and the *Teatro Nacional*.

The National Theatre, opened in 1973, is an impressive structure with an impressive reputation and an auditorium that can hold an audience of 1,600. Not only is it the home of the Dominican National Symphony Orchestra, but the New York Philharmonic and the New York City Ballet have perfomed here. Opening times for the museums are 1030-1730 daily except Monday.

Museum-lovers should be interested in the *Sala de Arte Pre-Hispanico Arévalo*, the Museum of Pre-Columbian Art at Av San Martín 279 on the second floor (third floor for American readers) of the 7-Up Building, open 0800-1200 Mon-Sat, free.

National Palace. The *Palacio Nacional* on Calle Dr Delgado (see Santo Domingo Downtown map for location), an enormous three-storey domed structure looking like a 17th-cent baroque palace yet built by Trujillo between 1944 and 1947, has been used as the seat of Government since its completion, replacing the Borgella Palace –

though until Trujillo's assassination 'government' was something of a one-man affair.

Rumour claims that Trujillo pocketed half the US$6,000,000 grant that was to finance the building, but it is nonetheless an impressive structure with a marble façade whose colours range from beige to pink. Appropriately, scenes from *The Godfather II* showing the outgoing Cuban President Batista's last night in Havana were shot in the mirrored Hall of the Caryatides (stone statues of naked female torsos) on the second floor (US third floor).

The palace is now open to visitors on a guided tour on Monday, Wednesday and Friday. Admission is free but by reservation only; ✆686.4771.

Botanic Garden. The *Jardín Botánico Rafael Morosco* on the north-west edge of the city in the barrio of Arroyo Hondo, covers around 450 acres (1.8sq km) and locally is claimed to be bigger than any such garden in the USA. Open 0900-1200, 1400-1800 daily except Mon, for nominal admission, the garden's main attractions are the Japanese Park, the *Pabellón de Orquídeas* (Orchid Pavilion) with some of the country's 300 species of orchid, and *El Reloj Floral,* (the Floral Clock). Access is along Av. J. F. Kennedy.

Other parks. The *Parque Zoológico* is a little to the north-east, and in the south the *Paseo de los Indios,* parallelling the Autopista 30 de Mayo, is a five-mile (8km) long park surrounded by some of the smartest homes in the capital, a distinct contrast to the slums in the suburbs. Its other name, *Parque Mirador del Sur,* hints at the good views to the south, over the Caribbean. And there's an Olympic Park not far from the Cultural Centre.

The Feria. Finally, the seafront Feria, which loosely translates as 'fair,' had its moment of glory under Trujillo, who staged the Dominican Republic's own World Fair here.

OUT OF TOWN

Faro a Colon. The mouth of the Ozama river serves as the city's port, but the tourist terminal for cruise liners, at Sans Souci on the eastern bank, is temporarily out of use. The main bridge, Puente Duarte, feeds outward-bound traffic into Av Las Améericas, passing the Faro a Colon, the incredible Columbus Lighthouse designed in an open competition by a student of architecture at Manchester Polytechnic in the 1920s, for which he won a prize of £5. Work began in the 1980s when the original plan was revived as a splendid symbol to mark the 500th anniversary celebrations, regardless of the faro's consumption of power in a land hungry for electricity. The building site was off-limits to everybody, but the entire nation was talking about the project, particularly after the lights were tried one night in 1988 without warning; the sudden appearance of a vast cross in the sky convinced many people the end of the world had come.

The Three Eyes. Take Las Américas highway east towards San Pedro de Macoris: just before the spur road to the airport is a wooded parkland containing *Los Tres Ojos,* the Three Eyes, some of the most beautiful caves in the country, formed aeons ago when their roofs collapsed. Watered by cool, clear subterranean streams, the *four* caves in the system have spectacular luminous green pools surrounded by whimsical rock formations of stalagmites and stalactites, enhanced by electric lighting. Steps – sometimes slippery with moisture – lead down into the caves, and a small boat takes you to the beautiful inner pool.

La Caleta Museum. Set in a park at the turning to Las Américas airport is a strange museum that is little more than a bohio-style thatched roof sheltering some Taino Indian graves which have been part excavated to expose their human contents. Visitors move along cemented catwalks about four feet (1.3m) above ground, offering a distinctly unusual insight into ancient burial procedures.

SANTO DOMINGO factfile

Hotels:

In the following listing, hotels are graded according to price, beginning with the most expensive. There are no 7$-rated hotels, and all those in the 6$ and 5$ rating have air conditioning, private bathrooms, cable TV, en-suite telephones, restaurants, nightclubs, discotheques, large swimming pools, access to sporting facilities, car rental agencies, business and conference facilities, babysitter services, beauty parlours, on-site shops, and live entertainment. Most of them also offer good views of the Caribbean.

6$

Jaragua, Av G Washington 367, ✆686.2222, Telex ITT.346.0758. 355 rooms; set in 14 acres of landscaped grounds.

Santo Domingo Sheraton, Av G Washington 365, ✆685.5151, Telex ITT. 256 rooms; the ultimate in luxury.

Santo Domingo, Av Independencia – Av Abraham Lincoln, ✆532.1551, Telex ITT.346.0033. 220 rooms; the most elegant hotel in Sto Dgo, beautifully designed and decorated.

Gran Hotel Lina y Casino, Av Máximo Gómez – 27 de Febrero, ✆689.5185, Telex ITT.346.0278. 220 rooms; city centre.

V Centenario, Av G Washington 218, ✆686.0000–40. 230 rooms; built for the half-millennium celebrations.

5$

Hispaniola, Av Independencia – Av Abraham Lincoln, ✆533.7111, Telex ITT.346.0033. 160 rooms; a twin to the Santo Domingo with access to its facilities.

KEY TO PLACES OF INTEREST

1 Alcázar
2 Culture Plaza
3 Enriquillo Park
   (for guaguas to E & SW)

4 Feria
5 Independence Park
6 National Palace
7 Olympic Centre
8 University

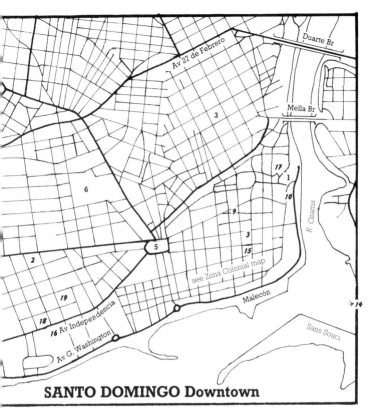

SANTO DOMINGO Downtown

KEY TO HOTELS
1 Caribe I
2 Cervantes
3 Comercial
4 Comodoro
5 Dominican Concorde
6 Embajador
7 Gran Hotel Lina
8 Hispaniola
9 Nicolás Nader

10 Palacio Nicolás de Ovando
11 Plaza Naco
12 Santo Domingo

KEY TO RESTAURANTS
13 Aubergine
14 El Bucanero
15 El Burén
16 De Ciro
17 Fonda la Atarazana
18 Jai Alai
19 El Toledo

Dominican Concorde, Av Anacaona nr Av Luperón, ✆562.8222, Telex ITT.346.0179. 316 rooms; a little out of the centre of town; one of the most comprehensive hotels in the Caribbean.

El Embajador, Av Sarasota nr Av Winston Churchill, ✆533.2131, Telex ITT.346.0528. 310 rooms; a renovated Trujillo-era hotel, spacious and traditional, set in gardens. Chinese management.

Hostal Palacio Nicolás de Ovando, C/ las Damas 53, ✆687.3101. Beautiful 16th-cent governor's house in Zona Colonial. Romantic.

4$: *the following hotels do not necessarily have all the amenities listed at the head of this section.*

Cervantes, C/ Cervantes 202, ✆686.8181, Telex RCA.326.4374. 171 rooms; family-run; central location.

Continental, Av Máximo Gómez, ✆688.1840, 689.1151–58, Telex ITT.346.0425. 100 rooms; tasteful but unpretentious; central location, good value.

Comodoro, Av Bolívar 193, nr Av Abraham Lincoln, ✆687.7141, Telex RCA.326.4202. 87 small rooms, popular disco.

Caribe I, Av Máximo Gómez – C/ Juan Sánchez Ramirez, ✆688.8141. 36 rooms; family-run, pleasant; central location.

San Gerónimo, Av Independencia 1067, ✆533.8181. 72 rooms; courteous and efficient staff but a little run-down.

Plaza Naco, Av Tiradentes 22, ✆562.3100, Telex ITT.346.0382. 105 rooms; near Plaza Naco shopping mall; pleasant commercial hotel, good value.

Napolitano, Av G Washington 51, ✆687.1131, Telex RCA.346.4101. 72 rooms; dates from late 70s yet already a little run-down. Functional; well-located.

Hostal Nicolás Nader, C/ Luperón – C/ Duarte, ✆687.6674. 10 huge rooms; beautifully converted 16th-cent house, period repro furniture; suffers electricity cuts.

3$

Comerciál, C/ Conde – Av Hostos, ✆682.8161. 75 rooms; traditional downtown hotel used by Dominican businessmen. Basic but clean.

La Residence, C/ Danae 62, Gazcue (S of Plaza de la Cultura), ✆686.2828, 682.4178. 24 rooms; old house converted, tastefully decorated; breakfast included.

Señorial, C/ Presidente Vicini Burgos 58, Gazcue, ✆687.4359. 13 rooms; family hotel popular with tourists travelling cheaply.

Ocean Inn, Av G Washington 555, ✆688.8242. 18 rooms; basic but well situated.

Hostal Llave del Mar, Av G Washington – C/ Santome, ✆682.5961. 10 rooms; located right in bustle of Malecón; restaurant below belongs to same management. Clean.

Independencia, Av Independencia 267, ✆682.5737. 10 rooms; beside Parque Independencia; convenient but noisy. Clean, hot water, private bathrooms.

Caribeño, Av 27 de Febrero — Av Duarte, ✆ 685.3167. 58 rooms, many facilities. Good value but in shabby part of town.

Tropicana, Autopista Las Américas km8, ✆596.8885. 45 rooms; respectable, clean, family-run. Pool, ✗, disco — but you need transport.

Apart-hotels:

Suggested renting for longer stays in the capital. They are akin to self-catering apartments or motel efficiencies and are fully furnished, often right down to the cutlery. Graded according to dollar-rating.

Plaza Naco, C/ Presidente González, nr Tiradentes, ✆541.6226. 220 rooms; new, good views. 6$.

Arah, Av 27 de Febrero 194, ✆567.4267. 24 rooms; luxurious. 6$.

Plaza Colonial, C/ Luisa O. Pellerano — Av Julio Verne,✆687.9111. 100 rooms; new, well-designed and located. 5$.

Drake, C/ Agustin Lara nr Av Gustavo Mejía Ricart, ✆567.4427. 28 rooms; AC or fans, near Plaza Naco. 4$.

Plaza Florida, Av Bolívar 203, ✆689.0151. 32 rooms; central, spacious and comfortable. 4$.

Bella Mar, Av G Washington 963, ✆532.4521. Good location but a little untidy. Small disco and ✗. 3$.

Plaza del Sol, Av José Contreras 25, ✆687.1317. 23 rooms; used by foreign students; convenient location. 3$.

Playa Real Hotel has its own palm-lined beach.

Turey, C/ Gustavo Mejía Ricart 8A, ✆562.5271. 19 rooms; one, two or three-bed apartments; pool, cafeteria. Near Olympic Centre. 3$.

Restaurants:

Santo Domingo has a moderately wide range of restaurants serving Dominican and international cuisines; among the latter you will find Central American, Chinese, French, German, Italian, Japanese, South American and Spanish. The country produces a good range of food at prices which are favourable to foreigners, and La Capital is consequently the dining capital of the republic.

Eating times. Dominicans eat earlier than most Latin peoples, therefore restaurants open for lunch from 1130, finishing around 1500. The evening meal is more flexible, with opening hours typically from 1900 to 2300 or midnight. Apart from the more formal and expensive restaurants there are many fast-food eateries and *comedores* in local style, where you can find a cheap meal.

Probably the widest assortment of restaurants is along the Malecón.

My list is selected from those that have a good reputation, and they are classed alphabetically according to style of food.

Arabian:

Ali Baba, Av Gustavo Mejía Ricart 79, ✆562.5191. Clean, unpretentious. 2$.

Dominican

El Burén, C/ Padre Billini 101, ✆685.7637. In old building in Colonial Zone; charming decoration. 4$.

Fonda La Ataranza, C/ Ataranza 5, ✆689.2900. Beautiful, romantic old restaurant opposite Alcázar. Courtyard with occasional folk shows. 4$.

Naiboa, Av Bolívar 703, ✆685.0902. Informal and attractive. 4$.

La Canasta, Sheraton Hotel (q.v. ➤), ✆685.5151. Open until 0600; Sancocho and Mondongo served. 4$

Aurora, C/ Hermanos Deligne 59, ✆685.6590. Good comida criolla in pleasant inner courtyard in Gazcue. 2$.

Vizcaya, Av San Martín 42, ✆689.3006. Traditional.

Comedor Independencia, Parque Independencia. Good location. 2$.

La Bodeguita del Medio, C/ Peynado 11. Also serves breakfast. 2$.

Comedor Marisol, C/ Mar/l/8a Montes 143. Behind National Cemetery; large helpings.

French:

Café St Michel, Av Lope de Vega 24, ✆562.4141. Creative meals, good service, pleasing décor. Naco area. 6$.

La Fromagería, C/ 27 de Febrero – Av Máximo Gómez, ✆567.8606. In shopping mall Plaza Criolla. Bouillabaisse, crêpes, fondues. 6$.

Le Bistro, Av Independencia 1353, ✆533.2027. Home-made paté and desserts. Homely, unpretentious. 4$.

Crêperie de la Casa de Francia, C/ las Damas 114, ℘682.1644. Fast, informal. Picturesque and historic setting. 4$.

German:

Aubergine, Av Alma Mater − Av México, ℘566.6622. 8 tables only; reservations; closed Sun. Authentic. 6$.

Gerds Hofbrauhaus, C/ Padre Billini, ℘685.9802. Bavarian specialities; small premises, casual. 4$.

International:

El Alcazar, Hotel Santo Domingo (q.v. ◆), ℘535.1511 ext 650. Gloriously designed, good value. Buffets from 1200-1500. 6-7.

Lina, Gran Hotel Lina, Av M. Gómez − 27 de Febrero, ℘689.5185. Wide range seafood and Spanish dishes; long established. 6-7.

Antoine's Sheraton Hotel (q.v. ◆), ℘685.5151. Elegant; good service, large seafood selection. 6$.

Mesón de la Cava, Av Mirador Sur, ℘533.2818. In a natural limestone cave, entry by 50ft (15m) spiral staircase; spectacular. Live music after 2100. 6$.

De Armando, Av Santiago 205, ℘689.3534. A former residence in Gazcue; seafood. 4$.

Festival Restaurant, Plaza Naco Hotel (q.v. ◆), ℘541.6226. 2$.

Italian:

The church of San Pedro de Macoris, a simple study of elegance, is dedicated to San Pedro Apóstol.

Italian:

De Ciro, Av Independencia nr C/ Pasteur, ✆689.6046. Converted manor house; music and entertainment; bar. Closed Tues. 6$.

Il Buco, C/ Arzobispo Meriño 152, ✆685.0884.
Narrow 16th-cent house; renowned for veal and pasta dishes. 6$.

Vesuvio I, Av G Washington 521, ✆689.2141. Traditional meeting-place; terrace overlooks Malecón. Popular; quick service. 4$.

Vesuvio II, Av Tiradentes 17, ✆562.6060. Similar to Vesuvio I but quieter. 4$.

Piccolo Gourmet, Av Abraham Lincoln 605, ✆566.6430. Casual, friendly; music. 4$.

Il Capo, Av G Washington, Hotel Embajador arcade, ✆532.9033. Quick and casual; pastas and large pizzas. 2$.

Oriental:

Jardin de Jade, Hotel Embajador (q.v. ◄), ✆533.2131. Elegant; decorated with ceremonial crowns and weapons from China. Peking duck a speciality. 4$.

Chino de Mariscos, Av Sarasota 38A, ✆533.5249. Typical Hong Kong family restaurant; authentic décor; informal, homely. 4$.

Restaurante Japonés, Av G Washington 513, ✆686.6566. Authentic; cook comes from Tokyo. Saké to drink. 4$.

La Gran Muralla, 27 de Febrero 218, ✆567.2166. Multi-level; popular with local Chinese. Sunny and spacious; good value Sunday buffets. 4$.

Lago Enriquillo, Parque Mirador, ✆562.8629. Inside park, busy on Sunday. 4$.

Lee's Kitchen, Rómulo Betancourt 2060, ✆562.8629. Down-to-earth; wide range of dishes. 2$.

Mario, C/ Mercedes 453, nr Parque Independencia, ✆682.3955. Popular, dependable; good take-aways. 2$.

Seafood:

Jai Alai, Av Independencia 4111 – José Joaquin Perez, ✆ 685.2409. Converted house; shellfish specialities, Peruvian *pisco* available.

La Bahía, Av G Washington, ✆682.4022. Grim exterior but considered one of the best for seafood; wide range. 4$.

Llave del Mar, Av G Washington – C/ Santome, ✆682.5691. Stuffed animals and fish décor. 4$.

Cantábrico, Av Independencia 54, ✆687.5101. Long-established; pleasant atmosphere. 4$.

El Bucanero, Sans Souci Cruise Ship Terminal, ✆685.1836. Beautiful view across river, especially at sunset. 4$.

South & Central American:

Asadero Los Argentinos, Av Independencia 809, ✆687.6792. Argentinian owner; good service. Roasted meats or mixed grill. 4$.

El Gaucho, Av G Washington 301, ✆685.0921. Outdoor terrace; live entertainment. Mixed grill. 4$.

Taquería Antojitos, ✆567.1118. Guatemalan; tacos and Central American cuisine; popular. 4$.

Spanish:

El Toledo, C/ Pasteur – Casimiro de Moya, ✆687.6343. Attractive, multi-level. Meat and paella. 6$.

Juan Carlos, Gustavo Mejía Ricart 7, ✆562.6444. Smart, top quality; wide selection. 6$.

Extremadura, Hostal Nicolás de Ovando (q.v. ◂), ✆687.0450. Lovely setting in beautiful old house. 6$.

Don Pepe, C/ Pasteur 41, ✆689.7612. New restaurant in old house; good décor. 4$.

El Bodegón, C/ Arzobispo Meriño – C/ Padre Billini, ✆682.6864. In Colonial Zone; typical Spanish, romantic. Closed Sun. 4$.

La Mezquita, Av Independencia 407, ✆687.7090. Popular, informal. 4$.

La Reina de España, C/ Cervantes 103, ✆685.2588. In splendid old mansion. 4$.

Mesón de Castilla, C/ Dr Báez 8, ✆688.4319. Popular and crowded; slow service. 4$.

Steak houses:

Bronco Steak House, Hotel Cervantes (q.v. ◂), ✆686.8161. Informal, open all night. 4$.

La Parrillada, Av G Washington 553, ✆688.1511. Fast service, casual. Out-of-doors, barbecued food. 2$.

Las Pirámides, Av Rómulo Betancourt 351, ✆533.0040. Popular, casual; nature décor. 2$.

Parrillada Don Miguel, C/ María Montez 97. Popular spot for grilled meats, 2$.

Vegetarian:

Ananda, Casimiro de Moya 7, ✆682.4465. Wide range; self-service, well-run; classical music. 4$.

La Terraza-El Terrenal, Av G Washington 47. Smallish selection. 2$.

Transport:

For bus timetable see Chap 7.

Guaguas leave the city for destinations all over the country; **northbound** travellers must go to the rear of Parque Independencia and catch a guagua at the gas station at the corner of Av Independencia. This will take you to the main guagua station at km9 on the Autopista Duarte. You might even catch a guagua leaving direct for your destination. For **all other destinations** travellers must make for Parque Enriquillo, half way up Av Duarte behind Av Mella and Av 27 de Febrero (see map of Santo Domingo Downtown).

Festivals:

The main festival is *Carnaval* when several days of celebration reach a climax on 27 February, Independence Day. It is a happy but wild occasion when thousands of people dress in disguise, the most popular being *El Diablo Cojuelo,* a horned Satan who rushes around beating the crowds with a bladder on a string. Up to 80,000 people squeeze onto the Malecón to join in, or to just watch the fun.

The Merengue Festival dominates the Malecón in the last week in July when all vehicles are banned from the area. Each band tries to be noisier than all the others, and the beer and rum stalls help the crowds get in the spirit. But watch out for the pickpockets.

Shopping:

The main shopping streets are in the Zona Colonial: C/ El Conde, C/ Mella and C/ Duarte; see the map of the area. The *Mercado Modelo* on C/ Mella sells local handicrafts.

Nightlife:

Santo Domingo has plenty of nightlife, but it's not concentrated in any one area although the Malecón offers something of almost everything.

The most popular, particularly for the young, are the many discos, centred mainly on the bigger hotels: examples are the **Neon Discoteca** in the Hotel Hispaniola, popular with the young, and the **Omni Discothèque** in the Sheraton, a more plush affair. Other well-

In the villages, collecting water from the local tap can take hours every day.

known discos are **Alexander's** at C/ Pasteur 23 for the young; **Bella Blu** on the Malecón beside Vesuvio I, for tourists and older types; **Alex's Club** and the new **Regine's,** both on the Malecón; **Club 60** at Av Máximo Gómez 60 for the young; and **Opus** in Av Independencia for a mixture of tastes.

Las Palmas in the Hotel Santo Domingo is an elegant intimate piano bar with live entertainment at weekends; the **Embassy Club** in the Embajador Hotel also has a live show. **L'Azotea** is a nightclub in the Dominican Concorde Hotel with live shows and dancing to Latin-American music, with panoramic views of the city.

The **Maunaloa** on C/ Héroes de Luperón at La Feria stages big shows from 2300, and reservations are needed: ₡532.3207. **Fiesta,** in the Hotel Jaragua, ₡686.2222, mounts a huge display of Las Vegas style glamour with dancing girls and tigers. Dancing girls and music are also available at **Xenox** at Av Ortega y Gasset 13, and at **Marabu** at Av Independencia 503.

Strip clubs? The most famous and expensive is **Le Petit Château** on Autopista 30 de Mayo, but there are others: the **Number One Night Club** in the arcade of the Embajador Hotel; **Via Ottorio** at C/ Felix Evaristo Mejía 6; **Mery Che** on the Malecón and **The Lido** on C/ José García.

You want something wilder? Here goes: **Club Felix Cachet** at C/ Evaristo Mejía 14; **Stargirls I** at Av Duarte 339; **Stargirls II** at C/ María Monetez 230; **Senado** on C/ Hermanos Pinzón; **Bon Soir** on C/ Juan de Morfa; and **Otro Mundo** and **New York Disco** on Av Isabel Aguir, #146 and #94.

Bars? There are many bars, catering for different clientèles and creating different atmospheres. For a sense of history and swash-buckling romance try **Drake's** and **Bloody Mary,** neighbours opposite the Alcázar. For a sophisticated atmosphere set in an ancient house there are **Raffles** and **The Village Pub,** neighbours in Av Hostos. Meet the yuppy (young, upwardly-mobile) set in the **Café Atlántico** on Av México and Av Abraham Lincoln and in **D'Golden** and **Ibiza** on C/ Roberto Pastoriza. For people-watching try the **Blues Bar** on the Malecón.

"Lonely young men should head for..." begins an advertising slogan, which goes on to list the **Manolo Piano Bar** at C/ Mauricio Báez 209, **Night Club Herminia** at C/ Felix Evaristo Mejía − C/ Máximo Gómez and the **Iguana Bar** at C/ Palo Hincado 128. I accept no responsibility.

Cinemas. There are many cinemas in Santo Domingo, often screening American films within three months of their release in the USA, keeping the original sound track and dubbing on Spanish subtitles. Box office charges are very low by European and American standards, but perfect projection is not guaranteed; you may have reels shown in the wrong order.

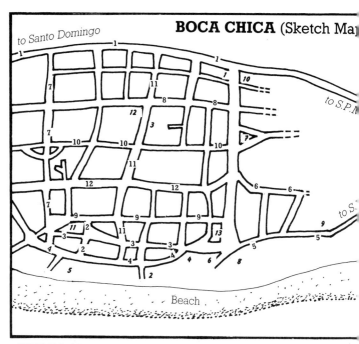

BOCA CHICA (Sketch Map)

to Santo Domingo

to S.P.M

to S.

Beach

KEY TO STREETS
1 Las Américas
2 Bernabe Hugria
3 Duarte
4 Abraham Nuñez
5 Prolongación Duarte
6 Prolongación 20 de Diciembre
7 Proyecto
8 Proyecto 2 DA
9 San Rafael
10 Sur
11 Juan Bautista Vicini
12 20 de Diciembre

KEY TO PLACES OF INTEREST
1 Aloha
2 Café Chocolate
3 Casa Pedro
4 El Cheveron
5 Don Juan
6 Golden Beach
7 Joy Disco
8 Neptune's Club
9 Sunset Beach
10 Taberna Alemana
11 Taxi stand
12 Villas Sans-Soucy
13 Willy's Bar-B-Q

Culture. For a more cultural evening, such as a concert or opera, the horizon is more limited. You have the National Theatre in the Plaza de la Cultura, where the *Orquestra Nacional Sinfónica,* the National Symphony Orchestra, is a regular visitor and reputed to be among the best south of the Rio Grande. For a programme of events contact the theatre box office (open daily from 0930) or go to the Palacio de Bellas Artes (✆682.6384) at the corner of C/ Máximo Gómez and Av Independencia. Tickets are cheap.

Casinos. Santo Domingo is getting a name for itself as one of the main gambling spots in the Caribbean. Most of the casinos are in the big hotels including the Plaza Naco, Embajador, Sheraton, Lina, Dominican Concorde, Hispaniola, V Centenario, and the largest of them all in the Jaragua. The Maunaloa at La Feria, in the south-west corner of the Sto. Dgo. Downtown map, is unusual for not being located in a hotel. Casinos are normally open 1600-0400.

BOCA CHICA

Eighteen miles (30km) east of Santo Domingo, the beach resort of Boca Chica caters for the people of the capital. At the weekends it is packed with bathers, sun-worshippers with radios and cassettes blasting merengue at full volume, and inevitably with other people trying to make a sale. The result to Euopean and American eyes is near anarchy. During the working week the beach is much less chaotic, and swimming and sunbathing are more enjoyable.

The sea is shallow as the bay is protected by a reef lying some distance offshore, and there are two beautiful tree-covered islands in the middle, giving a dreamlike quality to the view; Boca Chica's sugar mill luckily is a little beyond the western end of the beach.

Trujillo. Before the Trujillo era, this was a quiet little fishing village, unknown to the rest of the world. But Trujillo liked the place so much that he built a 30-room hotel, the Hamaca, with a third-floor (US fourth-floor) presidential suite for himself. The Hamaca is now in poor repair, but there are plans to restore it.

Boca Chica became a fashionable resort for the wealthy, who built their villas here, but with Trujillo's death Boca Chica opened to the less privileged and became the weekend getaway for the capital's masses.

The beach is a convenient place for tourists to see and appreciate Dominicans at leisure in their own land, with restaurants catering for all tastes from bargain-priced fish dishes to moderately-priced establishments for the tourists.

Accommodation spans the same range, from the cheap guest house to the smart hotel – and Boca Chica is one of the few places in the country where both types can co-exist.

Cheap eating. Boca Chica is close to the international airport of Las

Doña Nina's at Las Terrenas is at the cheap end of the market.

For something a little up-market, come to the Jaragua in Santo Domingo and sample 21st-century luxury.

Américas and is only a short distance east of the Sto. Dgo. − S.P.M. road which has a number of cheap eateries and discos that stay open late; for other nightlife head for Boca Chica's main street, Calle Duarte, which runs beside the bay and is marked by traffic islands at each end. The residential area of Andrés lies between the village and the airport.

Hotels:

Don Juan, ✆523.4511−8, Telex: ITT.346.0045.

66 rooms; a recently opened apart-hotel in a three storey beachfront building. Good décor; apartments have separate living room with ceiling fan and pull-out couch. Bedroom AC with private bathroom. Small balcony or patio. ✖, disco, beach bar, full ≈ with water-skiing, scuba, deep sea fishing. 5$.

Sunset Beach Resort, Av Duarte, ✆523.4808, 523.4616.

70 rooms and suites on six floors; AC, cable TV; pool with bar, live shows, sports; own generator; ✖ El Galeón on top floor with good views, seafood specials. Hotel is near eastern end of beach. 5$.

Demar Beach Club, ✆523.4365, 566.6011.

At western end; private beach; all ≈, ✖ and pub. Specialises in charter trips by boat for deep sea fishing, coastal sailing, cruising Ozama river. $4, includes breakfast + 1hr use of sport facilities.

Villa Sans-Soucy, Juan Bautista Vicini 48, ✆523.4461, 4327.

21 rooms, AC or fan. French-Canadian run, with bar, pool, ✖ for creole or Canadian food. 4$ includes breakfast and supper.

Terrazas del Caribe, C/ Sánchez 7.

27 one- or two-room apartments with fully-equipped kitchenettes; hot water. Bar, snack bar, pool, jacuzzi; beach 2 minutes walk. New. 4$.

Guest houses:

The many small guest houses offer cheaper and more intimate accommodation, and some are also restaurants or nightclubs. These are along Calle Duarte in the eastern part of the village: **Neptune's Club,** ✆523.6703, 3-room hotel, nightclub, bar, restaurant; **Hotel-Restaurant Arco Iris,** #50; **Hotel-Restaurant-Pizzeria El Cheveron,** #54, ✆523.4333, AC, hot water; **L'Horizon Hotel-Restaurant.** ✆523.4375, 3 rooms, Swiss management; **Hotel-Restaurant Paraiso,** #34, ✆523.4330, 6 rooms; **Restaurant Piccola Italiano Guest House,** #36, ✆523.4620.

Bar-Restaurant Techitos, Av Caracol; **Joy Disco-Restaurant,** also have rooms.

Pure guest houses are **Casa Pedro,** C/ Juan Bautista Vicini 49, ✆523.4773 and **Pensión Pequeña Suiza,** C/ Duarte 56, ✆523.4619.

Restaurants:

L'Horizon, ✆523.4375; overlooking the beach; thatched terrace restaurant in lovely setting; best reputation in town; fondues a speciality but many international dishes. Closed Tues. 4$.

Portofino, C/ Proyecto 3, ✆523.4660; Canadian-run with international menu. 4$.

Taberna Alemana, Av Caracol 15, ✆523.4649; German-run with German breakfasts from 0830; closes 2400; closed Mon. German menu or barbecue. 4$.

Café Chocolate, C/ Abraham Nuñez 13, ✆523.4263; Italian-run offering pastas and fish dishes. 4$.

Willy's Bar-B-Q, Av San Rafael 1a, ✆523.4344; casual eatery specialising in meats, especially ribs. 4$.

Plaza El Parque, C/ Juan Bautista Vicini – C/ Duarte; a small collection of several restaurants and shops opposite the park; useful place for a snack. Also a few apartments to rent here.

There are many small eateries along C/ Duarte, such as **Isla Bonita,** #48 and **Pollo Lindo,** #26.

Nightlife:

Small bars and discos are scattered along C/ Duarte, as already mentioned, and the search for nightlife in Boca Chica mainly involves strolling down this street where at #40 you will find the **Golden Beach,** a restaurant and disco, and in neighbouring C/ Caracol the **Joy,** another disco which might be to your taste. Your alternative is to explore Autopista Las Américas, the main road to the airport, for places such as the **Complejo Turístico Chuchu's** opposite the airport entrance, and the **Aloha Cocktail Lounge** by the Shell gas station at the entry to the village.

Transport:

Guaguas are easy to flag down on the main Sto. Dgo. – S.P.M. road for eastbound or westbound traffic, at all times of the day. There's a 24-hour **taxi service** run by the Tourist Taxi Office; ✆523.4797 or 523.4946.

16: THE EAST

Beautiful beaches

THE EASTERN PART of the Dominican Republic is fast becoming a tourist destination in its own right as it has some of the most extensive and beautiful beaches on the island of Hispaniola, washed by the Atlantic or the Caribbean.

The countryside is a flat plain to the south and centre, growing most of the country's sugar cane, with a low range of mountains across the north, a continuation of the Cordillera Septentrional.

Major towns. The major towns are San Pedro de Macoris, often abbreviated to S.P.M., La Romana, and Higuey; smaller communities are at El Seibo, Miches, Sabana de la Mar with its ferry to Samaná, and Hato Mayor. The main tourist resorts are Juan Dolio near S.P.M., Casa de Campo and Dominicus near La Romana, and on the coast south-east of Higuey the isolated Club Med complex, Punta Cana Beach Resort and Bavaro Beach Resort. La Romana has been overwhelmed by the tourist industry, but other towns are scarcely affected by it.

National Parks. The *Parque Nacional del Este* is near Boca de Yuma and *Los Haitises* is west of Sabana de la Mar. Another attraction, but far removed in concept from national parks, is Altos de Chavón, a mock 16th-cent village near La Romana that was the work of an Italian film set designer.

Roads. The coast road from Santo Domingo to San Pedro de Macoris, La Romana and Higuey, and the S.P.M. to Hato Mayor roads are in good condition. Those in the mountains and on the north coast can best be described as very bad, with the link between Macao and Bavaro being just a sandy track.

JUAN DOLIO (Costa Caribe)

The centre of Juan Dolio, lying midway between Boca Chica and San Pedro de Macoris presents a somewhat jumbled appearance with modern villas and condominiums built between the older wooden houses of the pre-tourist era. East and west of the village are the large hotels, a dozen or so as I write, but more being built, giving the village approaches an unfinished, almost transient, atmosphere.

Beaches. Despite these criticisms, Juan Dolio has beaches at its eastern and western extremities, right where the hotels are. A reef protects most of the sands, giving calm but shallow water for bathing, but with a sea floor that in places is rocky and uncomfortable. The resort's main attraction is its location, only 30 minutes from Las Américas Airport and less than an hour from the capital.

Coming from Santo Domingo the first sands you see are on Embassy Beach — its name is in English in deference to the tourist trade — a rather small and exposed cove with fairly rough waves which tend to attract body surfers. The next, signposted off the road, is Playa Guayacanes, longer and calmer, benefiting from the protection of the reef. The last sands are at Playa Villas del Mar, also known as Playa Real and Playa de Juan Dolio, east of the village on the road to S.P.M.

The region lacks a coherent centre, as Juan Dolio village offers merely the Plaza Quisqueya, a small mall of restaurants and shops which is nonetheless open 0800-0100. As a consequence the visitors, who are all-inclusive package deal tourists attracted by competitive pricing rather than luxury, tend to rely on their hotels for most things.

Hotels:

There are no small, cheap guest houses in the area, and all the hotels are low-profile resorts with tariffs that include all meals and drinks and, in some instances, cigarettes as well.

Embassy Beach Resort, ✆533.5401–10, Telex 346.0530 Embassy.

96 rooms, single, double or triple, AC, private bathroom, set in two-storey villas. Laundry, terrace ✗, pool, ≈, riding, golf, tours, auto-rental. Hotel is built on a coral promontory beside Embassy Beach; attractive but feels rather exposed. 5$.

Playacanes, ✆529.8586.

30 rooms with AC and phones, 3 suites with living room, bedroom, bathroom, kitchen, balcony. Two ✗, beach bar, small pool, tennis. On beachside; quiet, a little sombre. Beach is rocky and shallow. 4$ to 5$.

Los Coquitos, ✆529.8811, –4630.

80 one- and two-bed apartments; AC, cable TV, fridge, phone; ✗, pool, ≈, car and motor-scooter rental. Beside main road. 5$.

Decameron, ✆529.8531, –8631, –8432, Telex RCA.346.4144.

288 rooms. Big, ostentatious and pink, built around large pool which is surrounded by bars. Three tennis courts, children's activities, nightclub, casino; car and scooter rental. Beach is behind this well-run and comfortable hotel. Rates include three meals and unlimited drinks, 6$.

Metro Hotel & Marina, ✆529.8334, –8313, Telex 346.0243 Metro Hi.

180 rooms and 3 suites; attractive, new hotel by private beach set in coconut grove. Smart elevated pool; bohio bar on beach; two tennis

courts, ⇌, 200-seat conference lounge; ✕ El Puerto indoors, ✕ El Velero outdoors. Many tours on offer. Own marina. 6$.

Playa Real, ✆529.8471.

56 double rooms, AC; ✕ El Coral has good reputation. Practical, well-run hotel on private beach. P, pool, bar, bar service to palm-shaded beach. Many sports available but tourists seem determined to sunbathe. Piano bar disco, 200-seat convention centre; tours; auto-rental. 4$.

Sea Shells, ✆529.8210−1, −8251−3.

76 rooms, AC, ✕, pool; riding, tennis. 4$.

Costa Linda Hotel and Beach Resort, ✆529.8585, −8205.

132 apartments and 22 cabañas; all-inclusive package deal hotel; large pool, disco, tennis, children's playground, activities programme. Beside main road; short walk to beach. 5$.

Punta Garza, ✆529.8332.

46 rooms, AC or fans; cabañas or two-storey houses; kitchenettes. Comfortable but basic. 4$.

Apart-Hotel Marena Beach Resort, ✆529.8426, −8446, Fax 529.8835.

60 double rooms, 10 suites; AC, TV; rooms in attractive apartments in small blocks. Hotel is on both sides of road; seaward side has nondescript beach, landward has pool and ✕. 4$.

Talanquera Hotels and Villas, Country and Beach Club, ✆(Sto. Dgo.)541.6986, −6934, 567.2018.

140 rooms in a complex resort area; AC, cable TV; ✕, ⇌, disco, sauna, tennis, riding; car, scooter, cycle rental. Villas for rent or sale. 5$ − 6$.

Villas del Mar Realty, S.A., ✆(Sto. Dgo)542.7461, −7109.

A series of condominiums built 1988-1989 along Playa Juan Dolio. Condo blocks are called Yamina I, II, III, IV, V; for sale or rent. Each condo has two bedrooms, two bathrooms, kitchen. No extra facilities; short walk to beach. 3$ if rented weekly.

Restaurants:

All the major hotels have restaurants, and there are several independent eating-houses in the area. In Plaza Quisqueya on the main road is **Il Pirata,** for good pizzas and fast service; **El Coral** in Playa Real has a good reputation. **Allen's Restaurant,** ✆529.8668, between the village and the main road, was known for its seafood but the new Italian owners serve modest Italian food at less than modest prices.

Restaurante Casablanca, facing Playa Real Hotel, is an all-American steak house which is also good for seafood; ✆529.8111 for reservations.

Fast Dominican food is available from stalls along the coast, and there are a few comedors in the village.

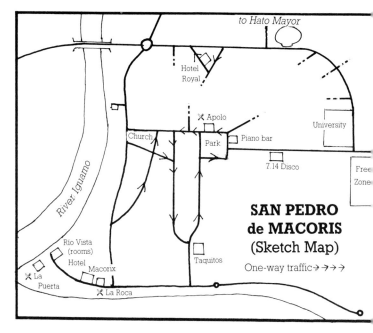

SAN PEDRO de MACORIS
(Sketch Map)

One-way traffic→ → → →

Nightlife:

The big hotels have their discos and piano bars, but for real devilry try the **Casino** at the Decameron; or there's the new and independent disco **Mágica Night Club** a few hundred yards beyond the Decameron towards S.P.M., featuring live music once a week.

Transport:

Wave down a guagua on the main road, east- or westbound. In addition to the auto-rental agencies at the big hotels, there is Budget opposite the Decameron.

SAN PEDRO DE MACORIS

San Pedro de Macoris — S.P.M. — owes its early 19th-cent origins to the mouth of the river Higuamo, which made an ideal harbour; it owes its past prosperity and former glory to the shiploads of sugar and bananas that were exported from this harbour.

Sultan of the East. This wealth financed the neo-classical and Victorian-style wooden houses which still line Av Independencia and which gave the town its alternative name, the Sultan of the East. To create these beautiful but now outdated homes, S.P.M.'s wealthy hired building craftsmen and labourers from the smaller British islands of the Caribbean; these so-called *cocolos* brought not only their ideas on architectural style, flavoured with the British Victorian influence, but also their own dances, the *guloyas,* and their music, *cainanés,* all of which have contributed to the town's unique cultural heritage. Come for the *Fiestas Patronales* on 29 June for a good chance of seeing the guloyas.

Free Zone. San Pedro fell on harder times when the world trade in sugar took a tumble, though three big sugar mills are still operating just outside the town. But S.P.M. today is gearing itself for another surge in prosperity, first by providing the housing and infrastructure needed for the planned Free Zone, and later by the wealth generated in the zone, which should employ 30,000 people, a sizeable proportion of the population which now stands at more than 100,000, and rising.

Baseball. San Pedro de Macoris is justly proud of its baseball players, and is the Dominican Republic's *numero uno* in providing big-league stars for teams in the USA and Canada; S.P.M.'s own team, *Las Estrellas Orientales,* the 'Eastern Stars,' draws big crowds to the Tetelo Vargas stadium during the baseball season which is from October to January, the opposite of the US season thus allowing American teams to come to the Dominican Republic for winter training.

Among those Dominicans who have made it to the big time in North America are Pedro Guerrero of the Los Angeles Dodgers and Tony Fernandez of the Toronto Bluejays. George Bell, a native of San Pedro who also earned a place on the Toronto team, was voted 'most valuable player' in 1987.

S.P.M. has its *Universidad Central del Este* which draws thousands of Dominican as well as foreign students; on a completely different level, the 1913-built *Iglesia de San Pedro Apostol,* the Church of St Peter the Apostle, also has its devotees though the tourist will admire it for its delicate structure and its riverside setting.

Out of town. The countryside beyond S.P.M. has two particularly attractive sights; unfortunately one is difficult to reach and the other is almost impossible.

The first, **El Soco,** is a beautiful spot for nature lovers, featuring a virgin estuarine beach. Add a variety of wading birds, a cluster of coconut palms overhanging the sands, throw in some land crabs, thousands of interesting shells, many butterflies – and, sadly, an assortment of insects. The water is a little muddy but the peace is magic – and the sunset is spectacular.

To get there, head towards La Romana. After the metal bridge over the Soco river, take the signposted track right and follow your nose for several miles through cane fields, to the beach.

The Cave of Marvels, *La Cueva de las Maravillas,* is so difficult to find that you need motivation — and luck — if you're to reach your destination which reputedly has many prehistoric paintings. The cave, also known as *Fun-Fun,* is eight miles (14km) up country; on your trials bike go to the batey called Las Pajas and then continue to Hoyón and Hoyoncito, where you'll need to hire a guide to take you on foot for the final five miles (8km), passing the source of the Almirante river which provides a refreshingly cool pool.

Hotels:

There are no tourist hotels in the town as only independent travellers visit San Pedro de Macoris.

Hotel Macorix, ✆529.3950. 28 rooms with AC. On the Malecón with sea views. Oblong, glass and concrete building that's not too bad; pool in front. Large P; disco, ✗. 2$.

Hotel Las Américas, Prolongación Av Gral Cabral, km1, ✆529.2349. 47 rooms in constantly-expanding hotel. AC or fans; generator, so hot water. 2$.

Hotel Royal, C/ Ramón A. Castillo 32 (opposite school), ✆529.7105. A collection of concrete cabaña-type rooms with AC or fans; reasonably clean; no frills. Small central patio for motor-bike parking. 2$.

Restaurants:

San Pedro has an assortment of restaurants serving good food at reasonable prices.

Apolo, C/ Independencia 53, ✆529.3749. In charming old building in Parque Central; the Chinese food is delicious with wide selection and large servings. Old-time sophistication — it's worth tolerating the occasional surly waiter. Good value. 2$.

El Piano. ✆529.2877. Opposite Apolo and similar in atmosphere. 2$.

Taquitos, C/ Sánchez, off Malecón. Mexican eatery with good local reputation, especially for snacks. Picturesque old wooden building. 2$.

There are many restaurants on the Malecón, usually specialising in seafood and creole dishes. They are pleasant with good sea views but are not the bargains named above. All are 2$.

Nightlife:

A good place to take a sundowner is **La Puerta** at the western end of the Malecón; it's a beautiful wooden multi-level bar-restaurant set above the estuary and with superb sunset views. It also has lots of tropical vegetation and a pool that's not always in use. Full marks for design — and it's not pricey either. From here take a stroll along the Malecón and listen to the pulse of merengue music from the discos and bars.

Nightlife ends in the **Disco Siete Catorce, (7–14),** half way along the road which links the park and the Free Zone entrance; 7–14 is in a building similar to a large house and has such an excellent reputation that men should consider wearing a jacket and tie. Its mix of Dominican and rock music makes it popular with couples, and the cover charge and cost of drinks keep it reasonably priced.

Transport:

Guaguas are driving through S.P.M. from 0600 to 1800, linking it to La Romana and Santo Domingo. They leave from the Central Park or can be waved down along Av Circunvalación (the main road running through the north of town), at the market or at the baseball stadium.

Nelly's Car Hire is at Av Circunvalación 9, ✆529.6768.

Festival: patron saint, San Pedro, 29 June; see text.

LA ROMANA

La Romana owes its origins and its early wealth to the sugar industry exactly as San Pedro de Macoris does. La Romana – its name comes from *la balanza romana,* the 'Roman scales' originally used for weighing the sugar exports – stands at the mouth of the Río Dulce and is still the base for the Central Romana Corporation.

Sugar. The corporation's sugar mill belches out smoke and vapour during the November-thru-July cane cutting season, most of the effluent blowing across the south-west part of town and away from the tourist areas. If you come during these months you'll also see huge rail

The Playacanes Hotel at Juan Dolio, seen from the beach.

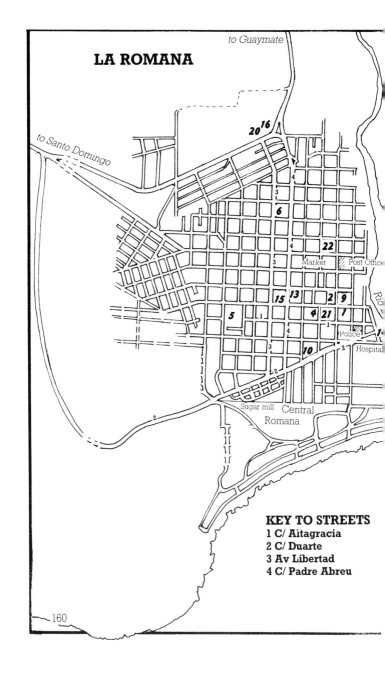

LA ROMANA

to Guaymate

to Santo Domingo

Market   Post Office

Río

Police

Hospital

Sugar mill   Central Romana

KEY TO STREETS
1 C/ Aitagracia
2 C/ Duarte
3 Av Libertad
4 C/ Padre Abreu

160

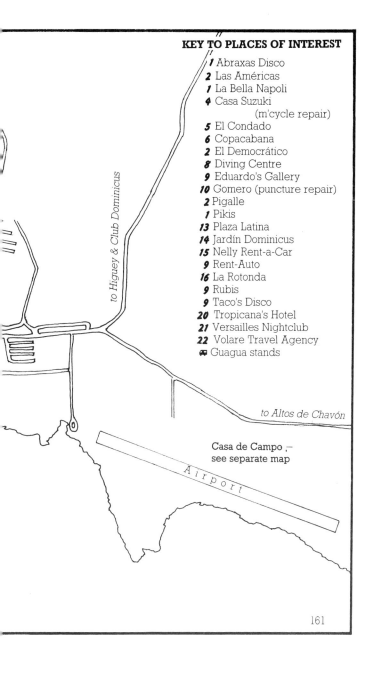

KEY TO PLACES OF INTEREST

1 Abraxas Disco
2 Las Américas
1 La Bella Napoli
4 Casa Suzuki
    (m'cycle repair)
5 El Condado
6 Copacabana
2 El Democrático
8 Diving Centre
9 Eduardo's Gallery
10 Gomero (puncture repair)
2 Pigalle
1 Pikis
13 Plaza Latina
14 Jardín Dominicus
15 Nelly Rent-a-Car
9 Rent-Auto
16 La Rotonda
9 Rubis
9 Taco's Disco
20 Tropicana's Hotel
21 Versailles Nightclub
22 Volare Travel Agency
🚌 Guagua stands

to Higuey & Club Dominicus

to Altos de Chavón

Casa de Campo –
see separate map

Airport

wagons rolling into the mill, laden with raw cane from the 107,000 acres (432sq km, 167sq miles) of cane fields that the corporation owns, for the Central Romana Corporation is one of the largest cane sugar producers in the world and responsible for a third of the country's output; it dominates the town physically and economically, and is the major employer in the eastern part of the republic.

Tourism. Yet the corporation's executives have sufficient vision to appreciate the need for diversification and, in addition to owning another 117,000 acres (473sq km) of grazing land, it has created the Casa de Campo tourist complex on 7,000 acres (28sq km) of what was originally scrub land at Costa Sur, east of La Romana; the entrance is about three miles (5km) out of town on the road that crosses the Dulce river.

Free Zone. And there's another source of income in La Romana: the Free Zone which now employs 8,000 people. Many of the inhabitants have been drawn in from the countryside and other communities by this economic magnet, but the sad aspect is that too many of them still live in shanty towns beyond the suburbs.

Growth. The tourist industry grows. Every year La Romana increases its stock of restaurants, bars, auto-rental agencies, hotels, supermarkets such as the Hilari Mayol — and even art galleries such as Eduardo's near the park. The town is 68 miles (110km) east of Santo Domingo, about a 90-minute journey by car, and sits on the flat coastal plain with its own airport only a short distance to the east; it is the ideal base for touring the eastern part of the nation.

Beaches:

The town itself doesn't have a beach: forget La Caleta and El Caletón which are too small, unattractive, and sufficiently isolated to pose a potential threat to lone women. Try first the nearest beach, **Las Minitas** at Costa Sur, whose sands were shipped in specially for the guests at Casa de Campo; if you're challenged at the gate you'll have to acknowledge it's officially private; if not — you're in.

Bayahibe Beach. Fifteen miles (25km) east of La Romana is Playa de Bayahibe which has all the ingredients of paradise: a splendid view, sparkling blue water that is deep enough for swimming, excellent white sand, coconut palms reaching out to offer shade, a coral reef for protection and for snorkelling around, and a bar-restaurant for cold refreshments or seafood.

The good news? As I write the beach is still unspoiled although each year it is becoming more commercialised. The bad news? Central Romana plans to built a huge hotel here.

Access. From La Romana take a guagua for Higuey and pay as far as 'el cruce,' (the crossroads), three miles (5km) beyond the Chavón bridge known as 'la represa,' then take one of the waiting motoconchos for the remaining six miles (10km). Access to the beach for people not staying at Casa de Campo is through the pretty little village of Bayahibe at the eastern end of the sands.

Accommodation in Bayahibe. The village has no hotel of any kind but at the beginning of the beach several private houses have been converted to guest houses offering simple accommodation yet with double beds, private bathrooms, mosquito nets and ceiling fans. At the other end of the village near the freshwater pool are some costlier cabañas, but if you let it be known in the village that you're looking for a room you'll soon be negotiating a price. Ask first at one of the restaurants.

Dominicus Beach. At the end of the tarmac road that continues past the Bayahibe turning, is Playa Dominicus and its related hotel complex, both often known as Puerto Laguna. The sands stretch for several miles to the entrance to the National Park of the East but at this remote end beauty is marred by the *jejenes*, those little flies with the big bite.

The first bay belongs to the Club Dominicus Hotel (see below) and you have to pay an entry fee at the hotel gate – but you can walk onto the beach for nothing from the next bay along.

Catalina Beach. I believe that Playa Catalina on Isla Catalina must be one of the best beaches in the Caribbean. The island lies just off La Romana yet is uninhabited: a Robinson Crusoe island that doesn't even have a Man Friday! To get there, go to the front desk in Casa de Campo to reserve a place on either *The Merengue* or the glass-bottomed boat, which sail to the island. Half a day costs RD$143 (US$23, £14), a full day RD$170 (US$27, £17).

Club Dominicus Hotel. The Italian-run Club Dominicus Hotel (✆566.4228, 686.8720, Telex RCA.326,4515, Fax 687.8698) has 120 rooms in pleasant beachside cabañas, with ✗ and bars. The atmosphere is European, with peace and quiet as the hotel is isolated beside a splendid beach; no wonder that topless sunbathing is the fashion. Riding, tennis, pool, car-rental; the hotel specialises in package holidays including all meals and drinks. 5$.

THE NATIONAL PARK OF THE EAST (Western Entrance)

Created in 1975, the *Parque Nacional del Este* has its western entrance around 30 minutes' walk from the Club Dominicus Hotel. Ask the warden – the *guardaparques* – for a guide to show you the *Sendero de las Cavernas*, the 'path of the caves.'

The path is a feature in its own right with many of its trees labelled in Spanish; look for the *cotonilla* which legend claims can make your flesh become puffy if you sit under it, and for the *caoba* and the *guayacán*, both treasured for their hard black wood.

The first cave, *La Cueva del Puente*, an hour's walk into the park, is a beautiful limestone grotto which is home to thousands of bats –

murciélagos – and which has large chambers of glinting white stalactites and stalagmites in many shapes and sizes.

You can walk back along the beach, where you can pick up complete conch and sea urchin shells. A final hint: take insect repellant and plenty of drinking water.

Isla Saona. Saona Island, covering 32,000 acres (139sq km), is part of the national park and has only one small fishing village. The beaches are fantastic, but it's difficult to get to the island cheaply. Negotiate a price with a fisherman in Bayahibe, making certain you both understand the figure and the times; Saona is at least two hours away so don't plan a cruise in rough weather. I recommend you also avoid the island in June when the sandflies are at their worst.

Despite the hazards, a visit to Saona will reward the keen snorkeller as the marine life is fascinating – and sandflies can't swim.

The Chavón Estuary. A rowing boat serves as the ferry across the estuary of the Chavón river, between Casa de Campo and Boca de Chavón village; in the latter you can hire a boat for a gentle fishing trip, or to row up the picturesque river to the base of Altos de Chavón.

Hotels in La Romana:

El Condado, C/ Altagracia 55, ✆556.3010.

12 rooms, basic, AC or fan but no generator; cold water; ✗, P; in quiet, central part. 1$.

Tropicana's Hotel. Av Padre Abreu 9, ✆556.2833.

22 rooms, AC; ✗, P; clean, modern; at top of town on main road to Santo Domingo. 2$.

Hotel Adamanay, 2km on Santo Domingo road, ✆556.2085.

23 rooms, one or two bedded; fan; private bathroom with hot water. ✗. 3$.

Hotel Roma, Av Padre Abreu, ✆556.2833.

22 rooms, one or two bedded; AC or fan; private bathroom with hot water; on road to Santo Domingo. 3$.

Apart-Hotel Libra, C/ Héctor René Gil 11, ✆556.3787.

9 rooms on 2nd and 3rd floors (US 3rd and 4th floors), AC or fan. Private bathroom; clean, quiet; near shops and market. 3$.

Daniel's Restaurant, see below ➡.

Restaurants:

De Américas, C/ Castillo Marquez 52, ✆556.3137. Successful. attracting tourists and locals; smart décor; food and service good, but servings tend to be small. Pepper steak is delicious; reservations recommended. 4$.

Don Quijote, Parque Duarte, ✆556.2827. Recently remodelled and now painted green; waiters dress elegantly; menu creole and international; establishing a reputation. 4$.

La Casita, C/ Fransisco Richiez 57, ✆556.5509. A converted house,

Diego Columbus was here. This is the Alcázar in Santo Domingo.

painted white; large windows give sense of space. Italian food; service leaves scope for improvement. 4$.

El Democrático, Parque Duarte. One of La Romana's older bars located right in the park; restaurant is behind the bar; food is good; popular with locals. 2$

Samir's Restaurant. C/ Castillo Marquez 37, opposite Pigalle. Typical wooden house, painted blue; converted into down-to-earth good-value restaurant by amiable Arab owner. Creole cuisine, good sandwiches and fruit juices. 2$.

Pigalle, C/ Castillo Marquez, 48, ✆556.3960. French restaurant, pleasant inside and outside but not a great example of French culinary delights. Not as busy as its neighbour. 4$.

La Cazuela, (The Plaza Latina Restaurant), ✆556.3107. At the top of this pink shopping mall behind the park; smart and formal; aimed at Casa de Campo tourists but hasn't yet hit the target. Spanish cuisine a speciality. Service is the most sophisticated in town. 4$–6$.

Daniel's Restaurant, 3 miles (4km) from Bayahibe on La Romana road. A beautiful two-storey converted house with split-level terrace offering good views. In open countryside 20 minute drive from village, so has own generator; Daniel and his wife run the place so well it's worth the drive. Arrive before 2100 and bring insect repellant.

Daniel opens cabañas for 16 people in summer of 1990.

Calle Duarte restaurants: El Piki offers rapid service and a choice of pizzas to eat in your rocking-chair; immensely popular. Opposite is the frugal-looking Chinese restaurant Rubis, serving cheap but uninspiring dishes. On a corner, La Bella Nápoli is a bar which serves delicious pizzas especially when the Italian manager is there.

Nightlife:

La Romana is a lively town after dark, particularly on Calle Duarte at the weekend. Here are the popular discos **Abraxas, Pikis,** and **Tacos,** all relatively trouble-free and unaccompanied women can go in with few problems. Abraxas has special theme nights including one for transvestites.

Away from the town centre the **Copacabana** dancing floor is at the corner of Teniente Amado García and Pedro A Lluberes, while **La Rotonda** is at the top of Calle Santa Rosa; La Rotonda hosts big-name merengue bands on Monday evenings.

There is no shortage of bars, particularly along Santa Rosa and the lower half of P. A. Lluberes, but for something quiet and romantic try **Le Jardin Dominicus** at the end of the alley beside the Casa de Puerto Rico; the casa itself was a club for Puerto Ricans running the local sugar mills but it's now a family club with membership by subscription.

During the October to April baseball season there is a lively atmosphere in the stadium on the road out to Santo Domingo; the local team is *Los Azucareros,* loosely translated as 'The Sugar Boys.'

Transport:

La Romana is well served by **guaguas.** Those for Higuey leave from the road beside the Ayuntamiento (town hall); for Santo Domingo take a free guagua from in front of the town hall to the guagua station on Av Padre Abreu.

For buses to the airport from Casa de Campo, and for tourist coach tours to Santo Domingo, Bayahibe beach, Ponce de León's home in San Rafael de Yuma, and the Basílica (Cathedral) at Higuey, contact **Tropical Tours:** the Casa de Campo office is on ✆523.3333 ext 3128, the office at the top of C/ Santa Rosa is on ✆556.1225. All coaches leave from the Casa de Campo (see following), with the US$10 fare to the airport giving a warning of the high cost of other fares.

Carros públicos run from near the police station — *la policía* — on Av Libertad to the Free Zone and to the entrance to Casa de Campo; the individual fare is less than a peso. **Motoconchos** cost a little more but will take you anywhere, but **auto rental** is the most convenient as public transport is not really satisfactory.

Festivals:

The *Fiestas Patronales* in honour of Santa Rosa de Lima are held at the end of August; the *Feria Artesanal,* (Arts Fair) is held in Altos de Chavón from 25 to 27 February, and is a good chance to buy local handicrafts.

Diving:
La Romana is a good place to go diving, for two reasons. One is the splendid dive along 'the wall,' the 100-ft (30m) underwater cliff off Catalina Island. The other reason is that Leo and Linda have a diving school here: ✆556.5350 calls their number at their home in Buena Vista Norte which also carries the diver's flag, red with a white stripe from top left to bottom right. Leo and Linda are PADI instructors and offer an introductory dive to get you into the water as soon as possible. By the way, if you're fully certificated, try a night dive in the Caribbean under a full moon — it's out of this world!

Riding:
Rancho Cumayasa, ✆556.3356, is eight miles (14km) out of town on the road to San Pedro de Macoris; if you're travelling west take a left turn just after the first river bridge, or ask the guagua driver to drop you off. The ranch offers riding on fine horses, and there's a simple restaurant.

ALTOS DE CHAVON

In 1978 Charles Bluhdorn had a dream. He called in the Italian architect Roberto Coppa and turned it into reality, the fantastic Altos de Chavón, an idealised version of a 16th-cent Renaissance village in the Mediterranean created with such attention to detail that the stone walls are built to look 400 years old beneath their cover of trailing plants.

In the heart of the village, surrounded by boutiques and gift shops, the Church of St Stanislaus is a little too ornate, but stand on the patio in front of the church and you have one of the best views in the Dominican Republic as the heights on which Altos is built drop steeply to the palm-fringed banks of the Chavón river, meandering down to the blue sea. By day it's beautiful, but at night when the lights come on, it's fairyland.

But Altos de Chavón has an even bigger surprise, a mock Roman amphitheatre with genuine Roman accoustics and seating for 5,000; many famous names have starred in concerts held in this open-air auditorium. The Museo Arqueológico, the Regional Museum of Archaeology, is in Altos with a glimpse of the country's pre-Columbian past, and the Altos school of art and design, affiliated to Parson's School of Design in New York, has a steady flow of international artists and medium-stay resident teachers who mount exhibitions in the gallery.

Altos de Chavón has come a long way from Bluhdorn's original dream and has survived Bluhdorn's death to become absorbed in the economic empire of the Casa de Campo, another result of the Central Romana Corporation's decision to diversify from sugar production.

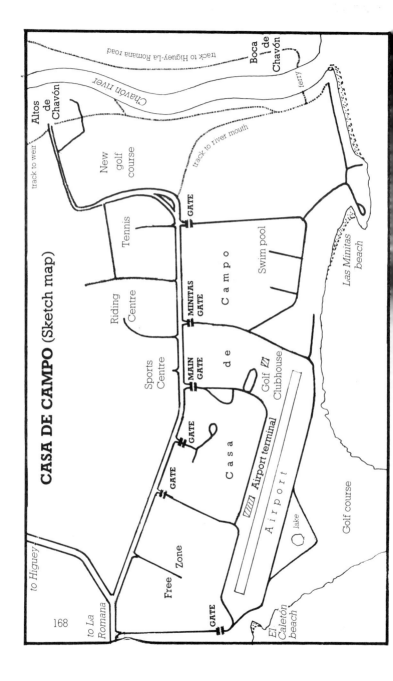

CASA DE CAMPO (Sketch map)

to Higüey

to La Romana

168

Free Zone

GATE

GATE

GATE

Casa

Airport terminal

Airport

lake

El Caletón beach

Golf course

GATE

Clubhouse

Golf

MAIN GATE

de

Sports Centre

Riding Centre

MINITAS GATE

Campo

Tennis

Swim pool

Las Mimitas beach

GATE

New golf course

track to weir

Altos de Chavón

Chavón river

track to river mouth

track to Higüey-La Romana road

Boca de Chavón

ferry

Hotel:

La Posada, ✆682.2111, ext 2315. 10 rooms; beautiful pool. Located just off the central square. 7$.

Restaurants:

There are several restaurants in Altos de Chavón with the emphasis on luxury and with prices to match. Starting at the 4$ end we have **La Fonda,** behind the museum, with an intimate Old World atmosphere and with chairs that don't let you relax. **Starei** is an option for the budget-conscious, a fairly popular Italian restaurant. For real popularity try the Mexican **El Sombrero,** where you'll often have to wait for an empty place at table; the Mexican minstrels entertain while a donkey looks on, bemused.

The **Café del Sol** is a beautiful terrace restaurant above the shops near the square, serving pizzas and light meals; 6$ but you're buying the setting as well. Also in the 6$ rating is **La Piazzetta,** a comfortable and sophisticated restaurant open 1900-2300, ✆523.3333 ext 2339 for reservations. The **Café del Río,** also open 1900-2300, and also on ✆523.3333 but with ext 2345, has the best view of all and is in the 7$ rating.

Nightlife:

Nightlife in Altos centres around the **Génesis** disco, a sophisticated place popular with tourists and the wealthy Dominicans. Music is Latin and rock, it opens at 2130 and the entrance fee doesn't reduce before 0200.

CASA DE CAMPO

Can you imagine a hotel resort that covers 7,000 acres (28sq km)? Can you picture a hotel resort that has its own international airport in its grounds? Can you then add one of the world's leading golf courses, a private beach, 13 floodlit tennis courses, a marina that has charter boats for coastal sailing or sport fishing? And can you finally add one of the most luxurious hotels in the Caribbean, with 794 rooms? If you can, you're beginning to appreciate the scale of the Casa de Campo.

This vast complex would be understandable amid the affluence of California or Florida, the Bahamas or the French Riviera — but this is in the Dominican Republic, one of the world's 'developing' countries.

The Casa de Campo, billed as one of the Caribbean's top-class resort areas, offers a wide range of activities but concentrates on golf and tennis. It has three 18-hole Pete Dye courses, the most famous of which is the 'Teeth of the Dog,' which costs RD$240 for a round.

Apart from the tennis courts the Casa de Campo also offers several pools, the main one having a bar on a central island and an artificial cascade feeding it. And then there is a fitness centre, a shooting range for the avid marksman, and four ✗.

The hotel has all the amenities you would expect of something in the 7$ price range.

Reservations. Casa de Campo is owned by the Central Romana Corporation but managed by Premier Resorts & Hotels, P.O. Box 140 La Romana, ✆523.3333, Telex RCA.326.4360 and ITT.346.0398. For further information and reservations in the USA, call the Miami sales office, ✆800.223.6620 or ✆305.856.5405.

Restaurants:

La Tropicana, ✆above, ext 3000. Open 1900-2300 nightly. In the central area of the complex and requiring a reservation. 6$.

Café el Patio, ✆above, ext 2265. Open 0700-2400; less formal than La Tropicana, offering snacks and light dishes. Near La Caña bar in the central area. 4$.

Las Minitas, ✆above, ext 2246. Open 1000-1700. A snack bar serving barbecued meat and seafood on Minitas beach.

Lago Grill, ✆above, ext 2266. Open 0700-1600. Pleasant open-air restaurant with view over golf course. Has a good self-service buffet breakfast. 4$.

PUNTA CANA

The countryside south-east of Higuey is poorer than average. The villages are small, most of the roads are bad, and cutting sugar cane is almost the only way of earning money. There is a steady population drift away from the region into La Romana and the towns further west, leaving this an underpopulated and underprivileged part of the country.

Yet there is charm and beauty here amid the forests and along the beaches, which stretch almost unbroken from Miches to beyond Punta Cana, the Domincan Republic's easternmost point.

And so the tourist industry has moved in. The resorts have no choice but to be completely self-contained and self-sufficient, attracting guests who are content to enjoy the sands, the sun, and the beautiful coastal scenery and have little contact with the Dominican way of life.

Airport. The resort complexes are Bavaro Beach and Gardens, Punta Cana Yacht Club, and Club Méditerranée, all served by their own Punta Cana International Airport which has scheduled links with San Juan, Puerto Rico, but takes charter flights from other Dominican Republic airports and Miami. It cannot handle long-haul jetliners.

Roads. The road from Higuey to Punta Cana is in fairly bad condition but passable by car; all other roads to the north are bad.

BAVARO BEACH RESORT

✆682.2161−8, 685.8411, Telex ITT.346.0159, Fax 686.5711

Possibly the best run and best located beach resort in the

Dominican Republic, Bavaro Beach is almost impossible to fault — provided you want the type of holiday it offers. The beach is private with perfect sand and crystal clear waters protected by a coral reef. Coconut palms lean enticingly to provide shade. And if you walk off the private beach you can continue all day and not see another human footprint in the sands.

This splendid isolation could be the resort's only disadvantage, but the little village of El Cortecito half a mile along the road has several bars to lure the tourist, and Transporte Bavaro has cars and motor-scooters for rent: a Jeep costs RD$570 (US$84, £57) a day, including insurance, with a 10% reduction for weekly rentals, and a scooter rents at RD$75 (US$12, £7.50) for three hours plus RD$15 (US$2.40, £1.50) for every extra hour. The hotel also offers excursions as far and as diverse as Catalina Island and Altos de Chavón.

Bavaro Beach had 2,002 rooms in 1989 with a 1991 target of 3,894. The rooms are built in well-designed blocks beside the beach, each with AC, phone, fridge, TV and private bathroom; there is evening entertainment, a beachside pool, tennis, all watersports, an 18-hole golf course under construction; and there are shops and an exchange bank. The hotel, managed by the Spanish-based Viajes Barceló group, specialises in budget package deals; day visitors must pay to enter the complex.

PUNTA CANA YACHT CLUB, HOTEL & RESORT

✆541.2724, 565.0011, Telex 346.0415 TREISA.

Punta Cana is expanding rapidly from its 1989 total of 100 rooms to a 1990 target of 600, set in 104 acres (42ha) of shoreline coconut grove. The building tries to capture the best of Dominican architecture set in natural materials, with accommodation either in single-bedroom apartments or two-bedroom villas, with AC and cable TV.

The large pool has an island bar; there's a ✗ and nightclub on the beach, a disco, four tennis courts, boutiques, all watersports, and the use of the new Punta Cana golf course, and the place emanates peace and quiet.

The beach is reasonable but prone to having kelp washed ashore, and the water is a little shallow, but a short walk takes you to a beautiful natural freshwater pool. 6$.

CLUB MEDITERRANEE

Reservations, ✆(Sto.Dgo.)567.5220, −5228−9, ✆(Punta Cana) 685.5500, −5532. Telex ITT.346.0550.

Club Med offers 356 rooms in apartments or bungalows, set in 70 acres (28ha) facing a beach that is protected by a coral reef. The complex, which opened in 1981, provides round-the-clock activities for its all-inclusive package guests who come in by direct charter flight from Miami to Punta Cana's airport.

THE RURAL EAST

With your own rugged-terrain transport or with tolerance towards a slumbering public transport system, you can explore the picturesque towns of the eastern interior, almost untouched by tourism.

El Seibo. The quiet, rural and totally unspoilt town of El Seibo comes to life in the first week of May with its *Fiestas Patronales de Santa Cruz del Seibo,* ending in a bullfight in which the animal is not killed. It has a decent **hotel,** the Santa Cruz (✆552.3306), a state run affair with 16 AC rooms with private bathrooms, hot water, a ✕ with a superb view, and a small pool. There's another ✕, Los Pinos, at C/ Gral Santata 53.

Hato Mayor. The roads into Hato Mayor are better, but the town itself has little appeal.

Sabana de la Mar. Sabana de la Mar lives by and for its ferry to Samaná (for details of the ferry see the end of Chap 13.) The state run **hotel** Villa Suiza (✆556.7304) stands in a field at the eastern end of Calle 27 de Febrero but has reasonable rooms, some with AC and all with private bathrooms, though water and electricity are irregular. The **hotel** Brisas del Mar near the quay is homely but grubby, although its seafood is good; you might eat here while waiting for the ferry. And if you are crossing to Samaná, don't look too closely at the condition of the embarcation quay or you may decide not to go.

Los Haitises National Park. Sabana is a good base for exploring Los Haitises National Park; ferries leave the rickety jetty for the park, or you could negotiate your passage with a fisherman. Los Haitises is a naturalist's wonderland, with a wide variety of flora and fauna, particularly the tropical birds. There are numerous caves, but as there are no facilities whatever in the park — it's almost virgin forest — make sensible preparations such as taking adequate water, basic first aid, a compass, and a companion. Knowledgeable guides are difficult to find.

Miches. The potholed road east from Sabana de la Mar goes to the sleepy little town of Miches where time seems to have very little meaning. Slumbering between the sea and the Cordillera Oriental, Miches has its own large but untidy beach across the river but, for a taste of adventure, ask around for a boat to Costa Esmeralda.

Staying in Miches? Then try the family hotel in the tall building next to the gas station near the bridge; the entrance is at the side near the bank. It's clean and cheap, and those rooms with a bath have water in barrels for when the power fails. Two family-run restaurants are on the seafront, the one further from the disco serves succulent seafood at bargain prices. And the discos are easy-going places to try out some merengue.

Costa Esmeralda. A 90-minute boat ride from Miches brings you to a little touch of paradise where you'll find four large cabañas with shower area, a generator for light and running water, and a small restaurant, built by a German-Swiss called Peter. It's an idyllic spot on one of the most perfect beaches imaginable, with the only access by boat. If you plan to make an advance booking and don't speak German, call Frank on ✆553.5344; he speaks English.

Difficult road. Throughout the east the most convenient way to travel is by trials motor-cycle or Jeep, but if you're relying on public transport you'll have little option beyond the ubiquitous guagua, except for the mountain road from Miches to El Seibo which is fit only for high-clearance four-wheel-drive trucks or bikes. This journey is well worth the effort if only for its spectacular views, but you should allow plenty of time.

Nisibón. The road from Miches to Higuey follows the coast for many miles, touching Nisibón, a pretty, brightly-painted village. The track is long and hard, but your rewards lie in the splendid scenery, especially if you decide to take your trials bike along the 35 miles (60km) of breathtakingly beautiful beach which I suspect is the most isolated coastline in the West Indies. On these beaches you are alone with the sparkling Atlantic, the acres of coconut groves and the miles of golden virgin sand.

Your trials bike can take you along the 12-mile (20km) sandy track that runs through the palm groves, parallel to the beach, and for pure adventure there's the self-operated ferry across the estuary of the Nisibón river, skirting Nisibón lagoon. To find this track from the Miches end, look for a cowpath from the road to the beach some miles before the lagoon.

The Ozama Fortress of Calle las Damas in Santo Domingo looks down across the river. This is the Tower of Homage.

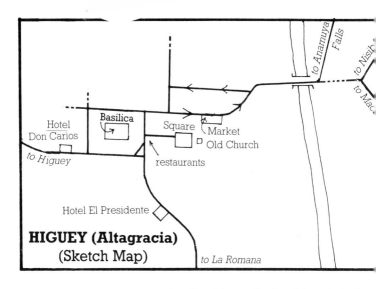

HIGUEY (Altagracia)
(Sketch Map)

(Map labels: Hotel Don Carlos, Basilica, Square, Market, Old Church, restaurants, to Higuey, Hotel El Presidente, to La Romana, to Anamuya Falls, to Nisib, to Mac)

Higuey. Higuey's attraction, for visitor or for Dominican, is in the Basílica de Nuestra Señora de la Altagracia, the Cathedral of the Virgin of Altagracia who is the country's patron saint. The cathedral was built in concrete in the 1950s and symbolises two hands clasped in prayer, a complete contrast to the 16th-cent Spanish church of San Dionisio facing it. Festivals and pilgrimages are on 21 January and 16 August, when Higuey becomes a spectacle of pure fantasy. A point of interest: the town's name in the Taino Indian language means 'land where the sun rises.'

There are several **hotels,** all family-run, small and cheap. The best and cleanest is perhaps the Don Carlos (✆554.2313) with single, double or family rooms with private bathroom and AC; look for it behind the cathedral at the corner of C/ Sánchez and C/ Ponce de León. It has a ✗, and one of Higuey's night spots, El Palacio disco, is nearby. Other hotels include El Presidente on the road to La Romana, Brisas del Este at C/Beller 28, and El Diamante in C/ Ponce de León.

More restaurants are opposite the cathedral, but none is above basic standards. **Guaguas** leave regularly for La Romana from the street in front of the cathedral.

Otra Banda. The countryside around Higuey is fertile, and the area is renowned for the painted wooden houses in the little villages. There is nowhere better to see these than along the road which leads east, through the small village of Otra Banda where every house and garden is striving to outshine its neighbour in colour and beauty.

You have a road junction in the village. East leads 11 miles (18km) to Macao while south-east goes to Bavaro Beach and Punta Cana. Camionetas that do the Higuey – Macao run leave from the junction of C/ Remigio del Castillo and C/ T. Guerrero D. Rosario, near the market; the journey takes about an hour and costs a little less than US$1. Male passengers can expect to be travelling in the back with the sacks of rice and plantains, a good vantage point for admiring the pretty houses.

Non-existent roads. *Do not rely on the mapa turística's interpretation of the roads in this area: the map is wrong.* Follow the routes marked on the map in this book.

Macao. Macao has a beautifully wild beach with moderately large waves, although the reef tempers them a little. The only places to stay represent the extremes available in the Dominican Republic, omitting the opulent tourist hotels.

At one end you have Don Coco's, three authentic, cheap, home-built cabañas right on the beach, with home cooking and the family to look after you. Draw your fresh water from a well, use sea water for the lavatory, light kerosene lamps in the evening, chase away the errant pigs, and build fires from driftwood. For the duration of your stay you can drop into the Dominican way of life; it's paradise for some.

Others may prefer the other extreme, Hacienda Bárbara (✆685.2594, 565.7176, or in the USA (516).944.8060), which looks like a mansion from *Gone With The Wind*. It has apartments with two double beds and private bathrooms and outside, landscaped gardens, pool, tennis courts, and a coconut plantation. A luxury hideaway – 6$.

Indian cemetery. The rocky headland on the east of Macao beach holds a Taino Indian cemetery where you might still find potsherds, or buy them for a peso or two from local boys. Beyond the headland lies the beautiful beach of Arenas Gordas – 'wide sands' – which stretches for miles up to the Bavaro Beach Resort. It's a beautiful but rugged coast, in places beset by currents that would sweep you away from shore.

If time is on your side you could walk this entire strand, but a Jeep or trials bike is more venturesome. Journey's end is the bars at El Cortecito village, already mentioned.

Ponce de León. In the friendly farming village of **San Rafael de Yuma,** 25 miles (40km) east of La Romana along a good road, you will find an unexpected museum, the 16th-cent house of **Ponce de Léon,** the Spanish explorer-conqueror who followed Columbus. The house has recently been restored and still stands in isolated splendour in a field so your imagination can create Indian faces spying on you from the surrounding forests. Ponce de León went on to establish the first

European settlement in North America since the Vikings – and he was killed by a poisoned Indian arrow in Florida in 1522 (see *Discover Florida* in this series).

Boca de Yuma. Further along the road is Boca de Yuma, a charming little fishing village whose people are friendly and welcoming. There are two restaurant dance floors on the cliffs above the mouth of the Yuma river, but for me the sea views are more impressive as I watch pelicans diving for fish; cross the river by rowing-boat ferry if you want to enjoy the reasonable little beach.

But Boca de Yuma has a splendid cave, the *Cueva de Bernard,* on the road west out of town, and in the jungle behind are caves which are even more impressive; no self-respecting speleologist should fail to explore them.

Accommodation? Cabañas del Este are on the road to the caves; 3$.

National Park of the East. Further along this track is the eastern entrance to the National Park of the East. It's possible to walk the entire 43 miles (70km) through the park in three days, but you would need to be in good physical condition as you must carry all your provisions except a tent – there are simple huts for overnight. The problem is that you must have a guide, and he won't be easy to engage; he'll find the journey just as arduous as you will.

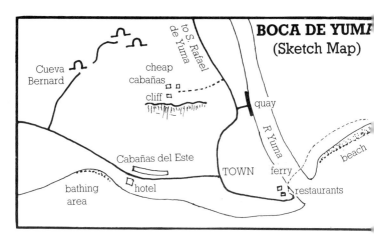

17: THE SOUTH

Adventure unlimited

THE SOUTH-WEST CORNER of the Dominican Republic is scarcely touched by commercialised tourism. There are no tourist excursions in air-conditioned coaches, there is only one small hotel-resort — at Baoruco Beach near Barahona — and travel becomes adventure. In this, the Dominican Outback, you are in command of your own destiny, finding your food at small Dominican restaurants or comedors, sleeping in Dominican hotels, and discovering at first hand a little of the Dominican peasant's way of life. The South is adventure!

Transport. For most of the area, only the basic guaguas and camionetas are available; in the really interesting areas, high into the mountains and deep into the valleys, you must again be self-reliant. For short excursions your feet are adequate, but if you want to explore this remote region of the West Indies, so unlike anything else you'll ever see in the Caribbean, hire a trials motor-bike.

Preparation. Make no mistake: this *is* pioneer travel, so you must come prepared. You'll need a reserve of food; adequate water in at least two carriers (one might leak or be spilled); goggles; protection against rain squalls and high-altitude chilling; a spare inner tube for each tyre, with puncture repair kit, tyre levers and a hand pump; a spare link for the driving chain, and tools for fitting it; a compass and as many maps as you can find, but don't place complete reliance on any of them; and a travelling companion on his or her own bike. A simple accident far out in the wilds could have major repercussions if there's nobody to go for help. And help, of course, could be many miles away.

Outback aspects. The South has several major towns. The well-surfaced highway from Santo Domingo serves San Cristobal, Baní and Azua, all attractive places that look surprisingly affluent and well-kept, especially Baní. At the end of the 120 miles (200km) of road is Barahona, sitting on the south side of the square Bahía de Neiba and marking the frontier to adventure.

Beyond Barahona a breathtaking and poorly maintained road clings to the flanks of the Sierra de Baoruco as it plunges into the sea; the views of the shingle beaches and deep blue waters are exhilarating.

The road passes through some poor yet charming villages to the coastal town of Enriquillo (not to be confused with Lake Enriquillo to the west) then crosses a plain to grim and desperate Oviedo, whose wooden houses are coming apart under the baking sun. From this, the southernmost town in the country, the dusty track turns north-west for Pedernales, on the Haitian border.

Back near Azua, another road branches north-west to San Juan de la Maguana, 46 miles (75km) away. This is a good road leading through fertile countryside between the Sierra de Neiba on the south and the Sierra de Ocoa, part of the Cordillera Central, on the north. You cross the Yaque del Sur river and pass through the valley of San Juan to reach San Juan itself, a large, bustling, attractive town. Beyond lies real adventure as you continue on a moderate road to Comendador, also known as Elias Piña, the gateway to Haiti and to the most spectacular journey in the Dominican Republic, the *Carretera Internacional,* the so-called International Highway which is in effect a gruelling track stretching from Pedernales through Comendador, north over the cordillera to Dajabon and the Yaque del Norte, and on to Monte Cristi on the north coast. Now that *is* adventure!

The journey to Lago Enriquillo is tame by comparison, but well worth the effort; the roads on the north shore are good, but those on the south are bad.

A final adventure is the road across the cordillera from San José de Ocoa to Constanza, an expedition possible only on trials bike as it involves fording two rivers and driving through pine forests shrouded in mist. You go through a region of haunting beauty and utter solitude, and though it's only 53 miles (86km) it will take you most of the day.

SAN CRISTOBAL

San Cristobal probably takes its name from the fort built by Christopher Columbus on the bank of the Haina river, several miles east towards Santo Domingo. On the Haina's eastern bank there are indeed the interesting ruins of a 16th-cent plantation and residence called Engombe, accessible from the capital along Av 27 de Febrero and Carr Engombe.

Trujillo. San Cristobal, 10 miles (17km) from the capital, is the birthplace of the dictator Trujillo, and it shows. Trujillo lavished a fortune on the little town, hence the art-deco style Hotel San Cristobal, the concert hall, and many other buildings which, one must admit, are well designed and built. Trujillo created the public square and the church as memorials to himself; the highly-decorated church, with its murals by Vela Zenetti, cost US$4,000,000 in 1946. But the dictator's mortal remains are not in the mausoleum as he intended; they were exhumed and taken to France.

Casa las Caobas. The dictator's manor house, Casa las Caobas, 'The

Mahogany House,' stands on a hilltop near the town, with a commanding view. It is now in ruins but, until the planned restoration begins, you can explore it for a few pesos. To reach the site, follow signs to 'La Toma,' which is the former dictator's private swimming area where three rectangular pools are watered by a stream. La Toma now has a disco-bar and a restaurant and is a popular meeting place.

Castillo del Cerro. That wasn't Trujillo's only grandiose folly. Another of his enterprises, the now-crumbling Castillo del Cerro, the 'Castle on the Hill,' looks down on San Cristobal. This place, which cost US$3,000,000, was so lavishly decorated that it was called 'quite possibly the most ugly building in the world.' It's also destined for restoration.

San Cristobal's beaches are Playa Najayo, Nigua and Palenque, which have beautifully clear waters; the town's *fiestas patronales* in honour of San Cristobal are from 6 to 10 June, and feature the *Carabiné,* the regional dance of the South.

Hotels and restaurants. Dominican hotels are El Caminante at C/ M.T.Sánchez 30, ✆528.3167; Constitución at Av Constitución 118, ✆528.3309; and San Cristobal at Av Libertad 32, ✆528.3555. A Chinese-Dominican restaurant called Wing Kit is at Av Constitución 79, and a little out of town on C/ M.T. Sánchez 13, is Restaurant Formosa. The restaurant-disco Magic Disco is on Av Libertad, and Lichy's Disco is at C/ Gral Leger 70. Codetel's office is at C/ Palo Hincado 15.

BANI

The people of Baní obviously have money. The town, 22 miles (35km) west of San Cristobal, is well maintained, clean and attractive, and has two neat parks. It also has a one-way system, which is a status symbol among small communities anywhere in the world, and will soon have that other status symbol of the poorer countries, recognition as a tourist destination.

Baní has a good selection of restaurants, hotels and discos, with some of the latter being quite up-market, and it's conveniently located not too far from the beaches of Las Salinas and Palmar de Ocoa, both of which face west into the Bay of Ocoa, while behind the town are rolling hills that lead up to San José de Ocoa.

And Baní, like San Cristobal, has a famous son, for here was born Máximo Gómez, who fought for Cuban independence against the Spanish.

Hotels. Near the first park you see when coming from the east is the Hotel San Martín de Porres (✆522.3583), offering airy rooms with private bathrooms and plenty of cold water; P for bikes in the courtyard; a bar that serves morning coffee. As with all hotels in the south, it is 1$.

Options are Hotel San Carlos at C/ Nuestra Señora de Regla 21, ✆522.3416; Hotel Alba, C/ Padre Billini 13, ✆522.3590: and others on the Carretera Sánchez, west to Azua, such as Hotel Caribani, #12, ✆522.4400; Hotel las BBB, km1½, ✆522.4422; Hotel Silvia, km2, ✆522.4674; Hotel la Posada, km2½, ✆522.4551; and the Centro Turístico Rancho Escondido, ✆522.4531,also at km2½.

Restaurants. Try La Gran Parada on the main road to the central park, for creole cuisine or a very good *caldo* stew. There are several pizzerías: Pizzería-cafetería Yarey is in C/ Sánchez; Restaurante-pizzería Santana is at C/ Máximo Gómez 5, and Mi Estancia is at C/ Mella 33.

Nightlife. For traditional nightlife you have the sophisticated Cachet Disco at C/ Padre Billini 21 and Night Club Oasis Video Centre at C/ Máximo Gómez 5, sharing premises with Santana.

The **Codetel** office is at C/ Padre Billini 3, and Baní's *fiestas patronales* are from 15 to 24 June.

Tourist developments. Baní's coastline has recently seen the beginnings of tourist development, with the hint that there is more to follow. For an attractive and peaceful resort, try **Boca Canasta Caribe,** a ten-minute drive from town where there are 12 apartments and six cabañas, with more planned; each has three double bedrooms, three bathrooms, kitchen, living room and terrace. The German owner and his Nigerian wife have a museum of African artefacts and hunting trophies, so no surprise the ✗ is El Búfalo. Pool; beach.

As I write the **Costa Brava Baní** is being built 170 yards (metres) from Los Almendros Beach, five minutes's drive from town: keep straight on down Av Duarte. This Costa Brava has a recreation centre with pools, dance floor, piano bar and restaurant, so far...

The biggest project is **Rancho Mar, Golf, Tennis and Beach Resort,** being built at Las Calderas, 11 miles (18km) south-west of town. It will have villas, hotel, apartments, shopping centre, a full range of sea sports and, of course, golf and tennis. Phase One plans to create 562 rooms.

BARAHONA

Barahona is an industrial town relying on the mining of salt, gypsum and bauxite. Although it's the largest community for miles around it doesn't have an air of importance but sits instead rather forlornly on the coast — but without a beach. It looks and feels a windswept town, built to confound any designer; even its Malecón is a strange mixture of open fields and discos in both directions, to Central Barahona and to the Pedernales road. If you're looking for beaches you'll need to take this Pedernales road, stopping off at Baoruco, Paraiso or Los Patos.

Hotels. Barahona has the state-operated Corphotel Guarocuya on the Malecón, ✆524.2211, with 22 AC rooms; it's a little dilapidated but is clean and functional, with a tiny beach of its own. 2$.

Other hotels: Cacique, C/ Uruguay 2, ✆524.2223, 2$; Hotel Yadira, C/ María Montez 20 (by C/ Anacaona), ✆524.3525, with AC in large single or double rooms; and Hotel Victoria, C/ Padre Billini 15a (by C/ Uruguay), ✆524.2392, with AC in double or triple rooms.

Restaurants. I recommend Las Brisas on the eastern section of the Malecéon; it is in a garden a little above the seafront and with good views. Seafood is plentiful and cheap, and the restrooms (toilets) are clean.

There are other eating places along the western half of the Malecón and around the park. The Malecón must be your destination if you're looking for nightlife as the discos and dance floors stay open until the early hours, but go to the park and the road nearby if you want to sample the bars.

Barahona's *fiestas patronales* are in the first week of October.

THE ROAD SOUTH

The real attraction in the Barahona area is the coast road to the south, where beautiful little villages cling to that precious margin between the mountain and the sea. Baoruco is one such village, and is now the centre of the **Baoruco Beach Club and Resort,** ✆685.5184, Telex 326.4248, designed to hold 90 hotel rooms, 85 apart-hotel accommodations and 34 apartments. It is being built on the fringe of a splendid beach between Baoruco and Ciénega and is being marketed at the wealthy. Facilities include jacuzzi, pool, ✗, bars, tennis, riding, ⌂, mountain and other excursions. It occupies a superb setting in lush vegetation near Barahona's International Airport, also under construction.

Alternatively, you can try the **Cabaña-Restaurant Miramar**, in Baoruco village, where you can rent a basic cabaña with two beds and a bathroom, but no mosquito nets. 2$. But there's little scope for eating in Baoruco.

The village of **Paraiso** has a small hotel on the southern exit; it looks like a house, is cheap, scruffy, has a communal bathroom, and is noisy. A plunge in the Río Nizaito may be more comfortable than the hotel's shower. Food in Paraiso is found at one of the *freidurias* where you take a seat in the street to eat your fried plantain, chicken, rice and beans.

Further south, **Los Patos** boasts a splendid beach that also has a cool, crystal clear freshwater pool fed by a mountain stream. The village is a base for exploring the seldom-visited *Cuevas de los Patos,* your last beauty spot on this littoral. **Enriquillo** is a dusty and unattractive town, though it has a gas station and several *pensiones,* but from here on the coast loses all its charm.

At the end of the road is **Pedernales,** a dusty frontier town which has the Hotel Noruega where a double room costs next to nothing. There's no generator, seldom any water, but you have candles, mosquito nets, and a place to park the bike. El Bohio is a good restaurant.

South of Pedernales is **Cabo Rojo** with its bauxite industry and a U.S. radar base. The coast from Pedernales to Isla Beata is a naturalist's dream as it's totally unspoilt, but security around the radar base makes access to the area rather difficult: that's doubtless one reason why the coast is still unspoilt. I haven't managed to penetrate this region but I think it may be possible by boat; I understand there are some large iguanas.

LAGO ENRIQUILLO

Lago Enriquillo is the largest lake in the Antilles, but it doesn't have fresh water. It is fed by streams from the Sierra de Neiba and the Sierra de Baoruco but as it has no outlet to the sea it's water loss is purely by evaporation. Its shoreline is unique in the Caribbean for being 120ft (40m) *below* sea level, a figure which fluctuates slightly during the seasons and from year to year.

Isla Cabritos. In the centre is Isla Cabritos, a national park, which is home to the Dominican Republic's only crocodile, *cocodrilus americus acatus*, and to many resident and migratory birds including the American flamingo. To reach Cabritos Island you must go to the house of the National Park's guard, two miles (3km) east of La Descubierta (look for a *cerveza fría* sign), where you negotiate for a boat and a guide. A recent price was RD$90 for the round trip.

Neiba. Several small towns lie near the lake's shores. Neiba is small but friendly, and its Hotel Babey on the main square has double rooms with mosquito nets and fans, but suffers frequent power cuts. The water supply is reliable (but not for drinking), and the hotel also serves basic but substantial meals. Access to Neiba from Barahona is better via Cabral and Duvergé, a road which has recently been surfaced; turn off the main road 3 miles (5km) north-west of Barahona near the garrison. The alternative road, via Galván, goes through several cane-cutting villages and is arduous, particularly in the heat of summer.

Duvergé. Duvergé has little to offer apart from a basic hotel, but the road from here to Neiba and on to La Descubierta is good.

La Descubierta. In my opinion La Descubierta is a charming village, possibly my favourite spot in the south. You can stay at the Pensión Marita for next to nothing, be it but a basic hostelry; you get a fan, and a girl brings buckets of water to the shed that serves as washroom; the toilet is in another shed.

But why bother? Why not follow the local people's example and head across the square to the cool, clear waters of a natural pool. Of course, the pool attracts other aspects of Dominican life, in this instance a merengue bar to liven the atmosphere and serve bottled beer.

Eating? I recommend Restaurant Brahmans for its good value, but you might care to eat from a *freduría* stall.

A final attraction in La Descubierta is the **Cueva Las Caritas,** the 'Cave of the Little Faces,' which has many Indian wall paintings.

Jimaní. At the western end of Lake Enriquillo stands Jimaní, an unprepossessing town presumably living off whatever advantages a frontier town may have. There are a few hotels, the moderately large one at the entrance to the town being dirty, noisy, and popular with the local garrison. Don't be surprised if soldiers stop you and search your vehicle when you leave town; that's normal frontier policy in these parts.

The road to Jimaní via the south shore is bad and passes through few villages, but it affords good views across the lake.

San José de Ocoa. Between Baní and Azua is the Cruce de Ocoa, the turning for the pleasant little mountain town of San José de Ocoa. The road, which is in fairly good condition, winds some 18 miles (30km) up into the foothills giving splendid views of the Ocoa valley.

In San José you can stay at the Rancho Fransisco, ✆558.2291, a small venture of 10 one- or two-bedroom cabañas with their own bathrooms. There are two pools, one olympic-sized, but the smaller is exclusively for guests' use; however, a dip in the Ocoa river may be more appetising. The family-run rancho is on the edge of town; 2$.

San José has a few discos and restaurants for your choice.

San Juan. San Juan is a surprisingly large and pleasant town living off the produce of its surrounding fertile fields. The Jaragua Hotel, beside the river, is reasonable, being the one concession to the idea of a stray tourist wanting to spend a night in these parts; alternatively you can stay in a cheap hostel. There is a good selection of restaurants and the inevitable discos around the square, which comes to life in the evenings as the town is the only focus of life for miles around.

THE INTERNATIONAL HIGHWAY

The International Highway, *La Carretera Internacional,* is a road purely for trials bikes over much of its length. Despite its grandiose name it is a dirt track, a mountain trail, and at times you might confuse it with a rocky river bed. It is, however, adventure.

The southern section from Pedernales to Jimaní is 59 miles (96km) long, but you should allow a complete day as the highway winds up the sierra beyond the 3,000ft (1,000m) contour before coming down to the Jimaní-Duvergé road. Don't try this stage alone; it's too isolated to warrant the risks.

Concluded on page 190

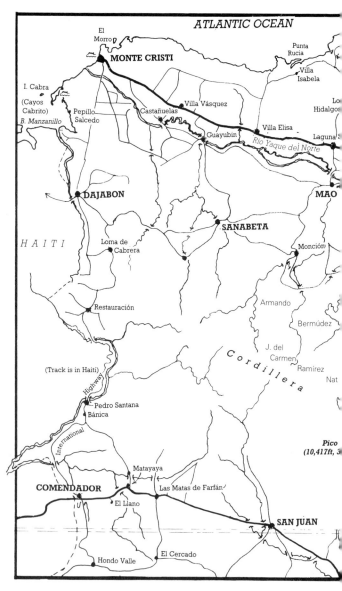

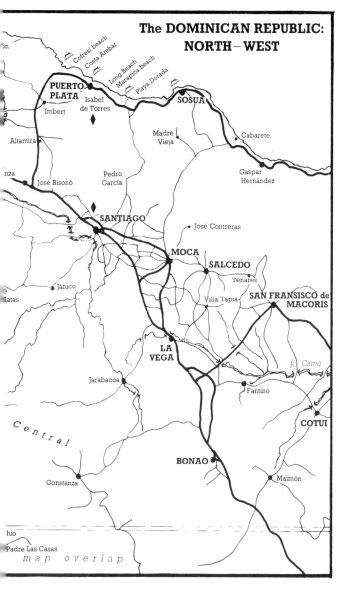

The DOMINICAN REPUBLIC:
NORTH–WEST

Cofresi beach
Costa Ambar
Long Beach
Marapica beach
Playa Dorada

PUERTO PLATA

Isabel de Torres

Imbert

SOSUA

ón

Altamira

Madre Vieja

Cabarete

anza

José Bisonó

Pedro García

Gaspar Hernández

SANTIAGO

José Contreras

MOCA

SALCEDO

Ténares

Jánico

s

latas

Villa Tapía

SAN FRANSISCO de MACORIS

LA VEGA

R. Camú

Jarabacoa

Fantino

COTUI

C e n t r a l

BONAO

Maimón

Constanza

hio

Padre Las Casas

m a p   o v e r l a p

185

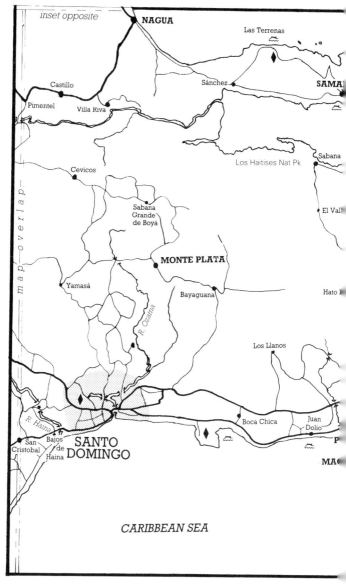

NAGUA

Las Terrenas

Castillo

Sánchez

SAMA

Pimentel

Villa Riva

Cevicos

Sabana

Los Haitises Nat Pk

El Val

Sabana
Grande
de Boyá

MONTE PLATA

Yamasá

Bayaguana

Hato

R. Ozama

Los Llanos

San
Cristobal

Bajos
de
Haina

R. Haina

SANTO
DOMINGO

Boca Chica

Juan
Dolio

P

MA

CARIBBEAN SEA

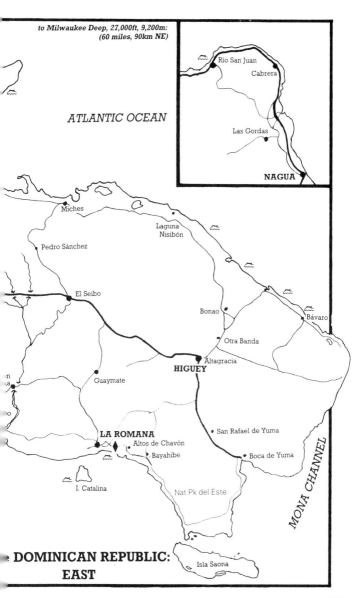

to Milwaukee Deep, 27,000ft, 9,200m:
(60 miles, 90km NE)

ATLANTIC OCEAN

Río San Juan
Cabrera
Las Gordas
NAGUA

Miches
Laguna
Nisibón
Pedro Sánchez
El Seibo
Bonao
Bávaro
Otra Banda
Altagracia
HIGUEY
Guaymate
LA ROMANA
San Rafael de Yuma
Altos de Chavón
Bayahibe
Boca de Yuma
I. Catalina
Nat Pk del Este
MONA CHANNEL

DOMINICAN REPUBLIC:
EAST

Isla Saona

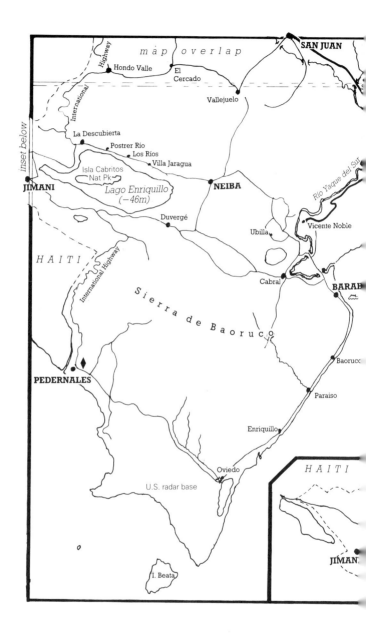

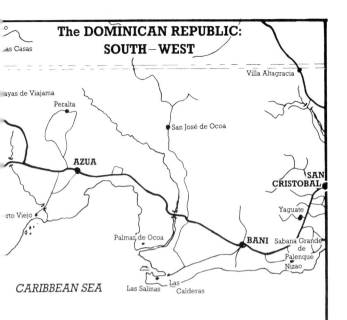

The DOMINICAN REPUBLIC:
SOUTH–WEST

Las Casas

Villa Altagracia

ayas de Viajama

Peralta

San José de Ocoa

AZUA

SAN CRISTOBAL

Yaguate

rto Viejo

Palmar de Ocoa

BANI Sabana Grande de Palenque

Nizao

CARIBBEAN SEA

Las Salinas

Las Calderas

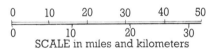

0	10	20	30	40	50
0		10		20		30

SCALE in miles and kilometers

KEY TO MAPS OF THE DOMINICAN REPUBLIC

— MAIN ROADS (Carreteras principales)

— OTHER ROADS (from 'good' to 'passable on trials bike only')

---- FRONTIER

⌣ BEACHES

♦ AIRPORTS

Continued from page 183

The middle section begins north of La Descubierta and winds its way to Hondo Valle where you can stay the night in a pension; you have another 23 miles (37km) to Comendador.

The northern section has no lack of drama, and if you are keen to try just this stage, come at it through San Juan, Las Matas de Farfán and Matayaya, where you must take the track to Pedro Santana. This sector is fairly flat, but make certain you have a full tank as the next gas station is in Loma de Cabrera more than 60 miles (100km) away.

The little villages of Banica and Pedro Santana are your last chances for a drink in a *colmado* for many hours: it took me nine hours of continuous riding from Matayaya to Restauración. You are already snatching quick glances of Haiti across the Arbonite river, and soon the track takes you over the river and the frontier so that you are actually driving on the Haitian side; you pass military command posts and realise that not all are Dominican. The scenery is remote but splendid, and for long stretches you feel you and your companion are the only people in the world.

When you reach Restauración you know you are back in civilization, and the great adventure is over. From here to Dajabon the road flattens and becomes easier, and as the day draws to a close you look for one of the basic hotels in Dajabon. Tomorrow sees the end of your journey, to Monte Cristi, where our discovery of the Domninican Republic began.

INDEX